WORKING
WITH YOUR
GUARDIAN ANGEL

1

WORKING
WITH YOUR
GUARDIAN
ANGEL

An inspirational 12-week programme
for finding your life's purpose

Theolyn Cortens

PIATKUS

ℬ *Visit the Piatkus website!*

Piatkus publishes a wide range of bestselling fiction and non-fiction, including books on health, mind body & spirit, sex, self-help, cookery, biography and the paranormal.

If you want to:
- read descriptions of our popular titles
- buy our books over the Internet
- take advantage of our special offers
- enter our monthly competition
- learn more about your favourite Piatkus authors

VISIT OUR WEBSITE AT: www.piatkus.co.uk

Copyright © 2005 Theolyn Cortens

First published in Great Britain in 2005 by
Piatkus Books Ltd
5 Windmill Street, London W1T 2JA
email: info@piatkus.co.uk

The moral right of the author has been asserted

A catalogue record for this book is available from the British Library

ISBN 0 7499 2585 X

Diagrams by Will Shaman
Edited by Anthea Courtenay
Text design by Briony Chappell

This book has been printed on paper manufactured
with respect for the environment using wood from
managed sustainable resources

Typeset by Palimpsest Book Production Limited,
Polmont, Stirlingshire
Printed and bound in Great Britain by
William Clowes Ltd, Beccles, Suffolk

We do not need a new religion, or a new bible.
We need a new experience –
a new feeling of what it is to be I.

ALAN WATTS
The Book On the Taboo Against Knowing Who You Are

Contents

Acknowledgements

Thank you to all my students for teaching me so much.

Thank you to my dear husband, Will, for supporting me in my personal journey – and for the diagrams!

Thank you to Anthea Courtenay for taking such loving care as the editor.

Thank you to the angels and invisible guides who have inspired this project; may it bring as much joy and delight to you, dear reader, as it has to me.

Angel blessings.

Prologue

The Infinite Passion of Life

*There is no end. There is no beginning. There is only the
infinite passion of life.*
FEDERICO FELLINI

When I was a teenager I saw a film that had a profound effect on
me. It was called *Splendor in the Grass*, starring Warren Beatty and
Natalie Wood. The story concerned two young teenagers in the
1920s falling in love, and going through the pain and angst that
teenagers always seem to suffer, whatever the social expectations of
the time.

The title of the film was taken from a poem written by William
Wordsworth, regretting the loss of innocence. In it, he says:

Though nothing can bring back the hour
Of splendour in the grass, of glory in the flower;
We will grieve not . . .

In the story the boy is above the girl in social rank, the adult world
of power and money intervenes and the young lovers are faced with
loss and heartbreak. They talk about Wordsworth's poem and how
they too were seeing the glory 'fade into the light of common day'.
The story, sadly, ends in tragedy when the girl goes mad and is
committed to an institution.

I was going through teenage emotional dramas at the time and

I could identify with this terrible sense of loss. But a little nugget inside me felt very rebellious. Why should we lose our birthright? Why should the heavenly vision fade? There must be a way to keep in touch with our natural wisdom. I had been reading mystical texts since I was 14 and I decided to try Buddhist meditation, in the hope that I would be able to recapture 'the splendour in the grass'. Even though meditation did not solve all my troubles at the time, it set me on a questing path – which eventually led to the writing of this book.

When I was 30, during a time of great stress, I was privileged to revisit that mystical state of consciousness in which we can see the glory of creation and realise our part in it. With the opening of my crown chakra (which was quite a shock, as I knew nothing about chakras at the time), I was able to experience everything around me in its full and amazing brilliance. I heard celestial voices and understood the inter-connectedness of all things. I felt the blaze of Divine energy rushing through all the cells in my body. Then I realised that we *can* bring the vision back. It is not, ever, lost: we have just closed our spiritual eyes and looked the other way.

After this experience it became my passion to live a life based on this vision, a life in which I could keep my vision clear at the same time as dealing with all those everyday things that make adult life so tiring; the routines and habits that encourage us to close our minds to the wonder of the world we live in. It is not easy in modern life to maintain an awareness of the kingdom of heaven within us. But a clear purpose and an open heart will allow us to create a life that we love, which will benefit the rest of the world. As Rudolf Steiner puts it: 'The rose adorns itself, in order to adorn the garden.' Our vision should be to live with passion, carrying a flaming baton like an Olympic runner, as a light for those around us, which we can also pass on to those who follow.

Theolyn Cortens
November 2004

that there must be something in it, because Pam always seemed to be able to cope with things that other people found stressful. When I told Pam that lots of people were interested in angels nowadays and telling others about their experiences, she was very surprised – and delighted to hear she wasn't so weird after all.

During the ups and downs of my own life I have become more and more aware of my own guardian angel and have developed ways of keeping in touch with this natural source of wisdom. I have always enjoyed sharing this knowledge, through writing and by developing a course, which I have now offered for a number of years and on which this book is based. This 12-week course takes you through a series of tasks, exercises and visualisations designed to open up your inspiration and to find practical ways of achieving your most heartfelt desires. It is divided into four parts, following a simple process based on the four elements:

FIRE Spirit: creative intention – reconnecting with your heart's desire.
AIR Mind: shaping your intention – understanding how your thoughts can help or hinder your unique life's purpose.
WATER Feelings: nurturing your hopes and dreams; learning to combat the power of negative feelings and nourish your self-esteem.
EARTH Action: making commitments and getting into action to manifest your purpose in the world.

If you work through these stages thoroughly they will lead you to a greater sense of your own power and help you to find a new meaning to life.

Finding a Sense of Meaning

In order to live happy and fulfilled lives we need a sense of meaning, a sense that there is a purpose, even when human lives seem so fragile and often shorter than we would like. Throughout recorded history, human beings have been asking questions about their own nature and about the meaning of life. Who are we? Where do we come from? Why are we here? What is the point of everything? Are our lives directed by our own purposes, or by larger forces, over which we have no control? Who is in charge, anyway?

When we are confronted with problems, illness and pain, these questions become uppermost in our minds. Down the ages, philosophers and spiritual teachers have grappled with these ideas and many of these sages have come up with similar answers, even though they have lived centuries apart and in different parts of the world.

All Science and No Soul

I remember when all my dreams were filled with light, filled with angels, flying free.
WILL SHAMAN

The most important question is the first: who are we? In recent centuries, since the development of rationalist and mechanistic science in the West, there has been a widespread view that a human being is little more than a complex biological and psychological mechanism. In this model, our thoughts and desires are based on needs arising from fairly simple biological requirements, such as getting food and reproducing. Nothing drives us except the 'selfish' genes, which just want to survive and replicate.

From this viewpoint, our ability to be moved by beauty, whether in nature or in the creative arts, and our potential to have spiritual experiences, are seen as mere by-products of a highly developed brain. In this design, there is no 'soul'; in fact, there is no design at all, since human beings have come about through a series of chance environmental factors. In the nineteenth century, the philosopher Friedrich Nietzsche announced that God is dead and the psychoanalyst Sigmund Freud told us that God never existed in the first place – we had just invented a father in heaven in our dad's image.

Today, more and more people are becoming dissatisfied with

these ideas, because they simply do not fit with their actual experience. People are aware of their own spirituality when they fall in love, when they have children, when they see loved ones die, when they nearly die themselves. Scientists, philosophers and psychoanalysts can theorise all they like but their theories cannot take away individual, personal experiences. Because these experiences are subjective, scientists find it impossible to replicate them and therefore dismiss them as invalid. When researchers investigate the paranormal, their interviewees often seem embarrassed, expecting to be regarded as cranks. However, I believe that nowadays people are reclaiming their experiences and are refusing to feel ashamed or anxious if their visions, dreams and intuitions do not fit with the materialistic approach of modern science.

Many people, even if they are not formally religious, believe they are more than complex biological machines and have a sense of having a 'soul', which continues once the physical body has ceased. This sense is reflected in the popular growth of the 'mind, body and spirit' market, including courses, books like this one, workshops and other events. Nowadays, a great number of people when asked the question, 'What is a human being?' would agree that we are physical creatures with a spiritual nature that is seeking meaning and truth. But if they were also asked, 'And who are you and what are you doing here? What is your individual purpose?' their answer might be a bit less certain. This book is designed to help you find your own answer to these questions.

Does Religion Have an Answer?

Although fundamentalism seems to be on the increase today, the more moderate religions, particularly in the West, have been waning in popularity. The idea of a Big Daddy in the sky does not work for us any more. In addition, many of us are put off religion by the constant squabbling about which faith holds the one and only truth. And when religions which preach love and non-violence then use violence to try to sustain their own status, it is no wonder people become cynical.

At the same time, ordinary people have been discovering that God (or whatever name we give to the creative power in the universe) is much closer to us than we have been taught. It is not only extraordinary saints and prophets who can receive glimpses of the Divine glory; poets like William Wordsworth have always seen the Divine in nature and conveyed that sense of spiritual presence in poems such as 'Tintern Abbey'.

> *. . . And I have felt*
> *A presence that disturbs me with the joy*
> *Of elevated thoughts; a sense sublime*
> *Of something far more deeply interfused,*
> *Whose dwelling is the light of setting suns,*
> *And the round ocean and the living air,*
> *And the blue sky, and in the mind of man.*

You and I, when we walk over the downs at the weekend, or when we are dancing, or gardening, or watching the birth of a baby, can have a direct experience of the splendour of the Divine power that creates and sustains us all. Even in terrible places such as concentration camps, people have had deep insights into the compassion this power has for every individual.

At the same time, all the world religions possess a wealth of inspired teachings, handed down to us from the mystics and saints who have recorded their experiences and struggled to understand and communicate them. According to most of the great religions, everyone has a soul which, in order to develop fully, needs to experience both joy and suffering. Even those who do not teach the idea of reincarnation describe the soul as being on a journey of self-discovery, whose destination is a state of spiritual peace – heaven, nirvana, paradise or the Buddhist pure land are not places but descriptions of a new state of glory. And on this journey we have a helper to whom we can turn for guidance.

The Guardian Angel

Beside each man who is born on earth a guardian angel takes his stand to guide him through life's mysteries.
MENANDER OF ATHENS c.342–292 BCE

Conventional religions have always asked people to listen to preachers or priests, read holy books and follow a set of rules in order to learn how best to live. But alongside this approach there has also been a mystical thread running through all the great religions, which suggests that the answers to life's problems are to be found within us. The only wisdom we need is in our own soul, the eternal Divine spark within us, and we need to listen to its messages. From ancient times religious teachers and philosophers have taught that each individual soul has a personal guide or teacher, the guardian angel. Just as God, in Biblical stories, used messengers called angels to communicate with human beings, our guardian angel acts as the direct messenger from our soul.

Although your guardian angel may seem to be a hidden and mysterious being, only making its presence felt when you are in desperate need, the guiding hands are constantly present, not to direct you like an over-protective parent – he or she only intervenes when absolutely necessary – but to keep an eye open for your best opportunities and to remind you where you are supposed to be going. Our guardian never sleeps. And if we stay connected to our angel, we will feel confident when making choices, and supported and protected as we move forward with our unique life purpose. And if you are not sure what that purpose is, this book, with the help of your guardian angel, will help you to discover it.

According to Jewish tradition an angel teaches the unborn baby the Torah while it is still growing in the womb. Once the baby is born, another angel touches its mouth so that all the teaching is forgotten and the soul will seek all its life to recover its lost knowledge. The sense that we knew something deeply important before we were born, and have to recover this forgotten wisdom and knowledge in order to feel whole and complete, is quite a common one. Wordsworth, in his beautiful poem 'Intimations of Immortality', describes how a baby arrives 'trailing clouds of glory' from 'God, who is our home', with an inner wisdom that is gradually lost as the child grows up, and the 'shades of the prison-house begin to close'. Birth, says Wordsworth, is 'but a sleep and a forgetting'.

This idea turns up in different cultures. The Greek philosopher Plato tells us that the unborn soul makes choices about its future life and chooses a daimon who will be its helper; then, as the baby is born into the world of 'necessity', the soul forgets its choices and has to rediscover them. According to the West African Yoruba tradition, before birth a contract deciding the future course of life is made with Olorun (God). At birth, all details of the contract are erased and are hidden in the *ori-inu* (the 'inner head' or 'inner consciousness'). For the Yoruba, life is a struggle to recapture the original plan and bring it back into memory, to provide a guide for living. Part of the process of remembering involves making a *ju-ju*, or a shrine to the inner head, as a way of trying to attune memory and destiny.

The course described in this book is designed to help you to remember your destiny and to reclaim your own inner wisdom and self-knowledge, by showing you how to keep in touch with your guardian angel.

Your Soul's Code

I do not develop, I am.
PABLO PICASSO

I have been a practising astrologer for many years and have observed how the life of every individual is the unfolding of a story based on an inner code. This code, which I call the 'soul's code', is the creative plan your soul started out with when it decided to incarnate into this life. It is a bit like the genetic code which decides whether a flower is going to be a daisy or a rose. Your task in this life is to fulfil your unique soul's code. This is not to say that everything is preordained but that we each have unique inclinations that tend to make us follow certain kinds of pathways. Your guardian angel has the job of reminding you what that code is and has agreed with you, before you were born, to help you fulfil your code and become the best possible human being according to that plan.

As I watched my four children growing up I became more certain that each person has a thread that they need to follow in life and that unhappiness (the root cause of all illness) is a result of losing touch with our sense of destiny. At the age of six my youngest daughter refused to go to school. Under normal circumstances she was loving, helpful and co-operative, so her tantrums when faced with school were quite out of character. When parental pressure was brought to bear and she did go, she promptly became genuinely ill, with various bronchial and asthmatic symptoms and, on one occasion, with pleurisy. Although she was bright and had no problems with school work (she passed a Mensa test with flying colours), it was clear from her natal chart that her inclination would be directed towards the arts, especially music or dance. We resolved the problem by educating her at home for a while and then sending her to a dance school. Then she developed knee problems and had to give up ballet. But she herself recognised that this might be another twist in her path of destiny. The dance school had helped her discover that she has an extraordinary singing voice and she happily turned to composing and performing her own songs.

By the way, although astrology is a good way to identify essential ingredients in your soul's code, astrological charts cannot describe the whole picture for anyone, because the chart cannot tell us about past lives and spiritual evolution. The course in this book does not specifically direct you to uncover past life experiences but you may have spontaneous recall of earlier lives while you are working with this material. Your guardian angel has been with you through many lifetimes, and during the periods between lives, when you were also evolving. So, working with your guardian angel allows you to gain a larger picture.

Becoming Master of Your Fate

I am the master of my fate:
I am the captain of my soul.
W.E. HENLEY

Since the development of modern psychology, we have been encouraged to believe that the personality is the result of a combination of nature and nurture. Child development theories tell us that our personalities evolve according to our environment and upbringing and that the events in our lives help to shape who we are. Even when we explore the notion of reincarnation and karma, we tend to see these ideas as locking us into a pattern of cause and effect, from which it is difficult, if not impossible, to escape.

When you follow the course in this book, you will be working from a different standpoint, which will make you feel much more powerful. According to this view, *each individual is the cause of all the effects in his or her life.* Even if you are unaware of the creative power you possess to make things happen around you and for you, nonetheless every thought you think has the potential to unfold into reality – your reality. The Buddhists say that we create the world out of our thoughts – so we had better be careful what we think. But an important question follows from this – where do our thoughts come from?

Your thoughts come from your essence, from your core being. Just as an oak develops from the acorn, which carries the oak's 'code', everything that happens in your story is a direct reflection of your inner being. Because the soul's code, just like the code in our DNA, came into being before we had access to language and verbal understanding, it can be difficult for us to get an overview of ourselves. Often things just seem to happen *to* us and events around us seem beyond our control. But the truth is that every thought we have, even those thoughts we are not consciously aware of, are shaping the lives we are leading. We are creating our own destiny.

Deep within your heart is a Divine spark, a fragment of the Divine whole, which has the power to create events, or to set up relationships with particular people, in order to bring your true self to its full potential. At a subtle level you are constantly making choices about your destiny and co-creating the events in your unique story. The more conscious of the plot you become, the better informed you will be and the wiser your choices will be. Meanwhile, your guardian angel is carrying the script around, like a personal assistant to a film director. At the same time, he or she is putting things your way, to remind you of your own story-line. She or he will not only save you from disasters, like fatal accidents (provided it is not your time to die), but will also create opportunities for you to discover who you are. In your lifetime you may have experienced some events as challenging, if not downright tough. But, while you are working through this course, you will gradually discover that each of these difficult lessons is a valuable step towards wisdom. You may not feel the Divine spark shining in your life at present but during these 12 weeks you will cement your relationship with your own guardian angel and you will feel more confident, knowing that you have constant access to Divine wisdom and support.

Navigating the Seas of Life

When the soul wants to experience something it throws an image of the experience out before it and enters into its own image.
MEISTER ECKHART

If you are the 'captain of your soul', then the guardian angel is your navigator, guiding you across the ocean of life, through calm or choppy seas. And, it has often been said, calm seas do not make skilful sailors. The guardian angel is like a magnet, like the compass or lodestar used by sailors, drawing us towards people and situations which provide us with the opportunities we need for growth.

The ocean is a useful metaphor when we talk about life's journey, partly because it has the potential to be stormy and dangerous, as well as beautiful, like human life, and also because it is deep and mysterious, like our consciousness. Similarly, our journey can take us to exciting places across the sea, or we can choose to stay safely in harbour. If we play safe and do not explore life's possibilities, we may come to the end of our lifespan wishing we had been more adventurous. Tapping in to the wisdom of our guardian angel enables us to make maps of unknown territories and discover new continents. But – there is no travel insurance as a safety net on this voyage!

The Freedom to Be

I am free when I am within myself.
G.W.F. HEGEL

If your whole life is based on fitting into the patterns and expectations of other people, or of society, then you have no real freedom to *be*. When we allow circumstances, social forces or other people to dictate how we are, then we lose touch with our own soul. But when you find the essence of yourself within yourself, then you are truly whole. This is a place of strength and power from which you can make real choices, fundamental choices, based on inner freedom and self-knowledge.

Most of the significant people in human history have acted from an inner conviction that something within us was superior to circumstances and that this inner power had the ability to change or direct events to our benefit. The person who listens to the inner voice of the guardian angel may seem to 'dance to a different drum'; she or he may seem eccentric and sometimes 'difficult' or 'unreasonable' but, to live joyfully, that inner call must be answered.

When you look at the life of any remarkable person, the kind of person whose name goes into the history books, you may think, 'That's all very well, but that's not me. I don't expect to be extraordinary.' But the only reason a few people are recognised as unusual or special is because most of us don't live our lives to the full. One of the reasons humans shy away from standing out in the crowd is fear – fear of ridicule, fear of failure, fear of reprisal. It is easier, safer and less demanding to muddle along, taking what comes and allowing the ebb and flow of life to take us where it chooses, rather than taking charge and directing our own ships.

According to the writer George Bernard Shaw: 'The reasonable man adapts himself to the world: the unreasonable one persists in trying to adapt the world to himself. Therefore, all progress depends on the unreasonable man.' There are plenty of examples of 'unreasonable men' to choose from – and don't think that it is only men who have followed their thread of destiny without flinching. Think of all the 'unreasonable' women – Hildegard of Bingen, Joan of Arc, Teresa of Avila, Florence Nightingale, Emily Pankhurst, Anne Besant (not only a great esoteric thinker but a champion for women), Lily Montagu (the first Jewish woman to be recognised as a minister), Germaine Greer . . . we could go on. Shaw is right, without people like these – men or women – human beings would not make progress.

Taking the Helm

If there is a way through, I will find it. If there is no way through I will make one.
HANNIBAL, who crossed the Alps with elephants

The course in this book is designed to put you back at the helm of your soul ship and to teach you the skills for steering. You need a map and the courage and determination to follow your soul's journey, even if it means taking some radical steps to change your present lifestyle. As you work through the exercises you will discover you have more gifts, talents and wisdom than you suspected and you will feel inspired to find ways to share these with others. When you realign your life with your original intention – your soul's code – a new enthusiasm will arise in you, a passionate commitment to fulfil your own destiny. This passion creates a magical force field around you, which will attract what you need and will protect you from harm. Above all, you will discover that you have a friend, an inner navigator, who will help you make wise choices and will be your cheerleader when things seem tough. This is your guardian angel; your Divine life coach and mentor.

Getting Started

The greatest thing in the world is to know how to be oneself.
MONTAIGNE

You are about to embark on an important journey. This chapter sets out the aims of the course and describes the working methods you will be using, so please read it carefully before starting any of the activities.

This course is designed to change the way you experience your life. If you do not already have a powerful connection to your guardian angel, you will be developing this as you work through the tasks with your guardian at your side. During the next 12 weeks you will be working through a series of exercises, visualisations, activities and research assignments, all carefully designed to help you uncover your soul's code and then to help you act on your newly found knowledge. If you have already done some spiritual work, some aspects of this code may be well known to you, but this book will encourage new insights and you will see more clearly how different aspects of your life fit together.

Some of the exercises ask you to delve deeply into your own inner world, others are light-hearted and simple, but they are all designed to help you reach a position of power, so that you will feel confident about your direction in life. Each week you will be growing in confidence as changes unfold in your everyday life. I shall be asking you to set aside an evening a week and to be prepared to think about the material, or do research projects, during the days in between.

The course unfolds through four carefully planned stages, with three weeks' work in each section. The stages are based on traditional wisdom, which identifies a fourfold process in creation.

The Four Stages of Creation

In order to manifest anything, whether it be a baby, a plant, a book or a job, four distinct stages are involved:

1. Creative intention: desire, will, enthusiasm, vision.
2. Information: design, decisions and choices, planning and organisation.
3. Nurturing: loving care, positive attention, gestation.
4. Manifestation: action, protection, stewardship.

Ancient cosmology related these four stages to the four elements: Fire, Air, Water and Earth.

The first stage takes place in the world of creative intention: fire. In this stage the Divine will initiates the created universe out of its own passionate desire to manifest its invisible glory.

During this stage (Weeks 1–3), your first task will be to establish, or re-establish, contact with your guardian angel, who is your Divine life coach. A visualisation for this is given on page 23 at the end of this chapter. A vital part of the course is keeping in touch with your guardian angel, checking in with him or her at least once each week.

The second stage occurs in the world of information: air. Here, the initial impulse is processed and shaped in the form of ideas. If we do not have an idea of what is going to be manifested, the next two stages cannot unfold. In this stage, your guardian angel will help you to sort your ideas, so that you can identify the most powerful possibilities to develop, in order to start manifesting your heart's desire.

In this section (Weeks 4–6) you will be uncovering your basic purpose and learning how your thoughts shape your destiny. Carving your way through what I call 'thought brambles' will allow you to clear the way for making a fresh start in difficult aspects of your life. You will look at choices you have made in the past and discover that making new choices can help you to realign your everyday life with your true purpose.

The third stage develops in the world of nurturing: water. Just as a baby spends several months in water, as the idea of its being unfolds through the early stages of life, so all creative projects need nurturing, time and patience. Every seed contains the idea of the plant it will become; the gardener nurtures the seed in its early stages, giving it tender loving care, as well as water and nutrients. During this three-week block (Weeks 7–9) your guardian angel helps you to heal old wounds, deal with emotional gremlins and find ways to nurture yourself, so that your life purpose can flourish in the world.

The fourth stage brings the invisible into the visible, sensory world of manifestation: Earth. The initial impulse can now, finally, be seen and measured in the real world. In this stage, we have to maintain our project or product, so that it can be useful, or beautiful, and can be sustained for as long as is appropriate.

During this final stage (Weeks 10–12) you will be acting in the world to manifest your true purpose, which is your soul's true desire, and will begin to see results in all kinds of areas of your life: your relationships, your finances, your health, your career. Your guardian angel will be reminding you of your commitment and will be there to support you when you find the going tough.

The Creative Process

The philosophers of the past imagined this process as a series of concentric circles around an inner point which represented the source of creativity (see Figure 1 opposite).

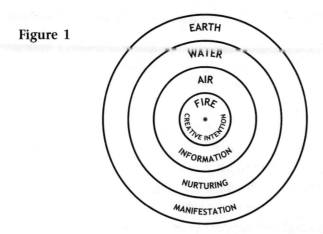

Figure 1

Figure 2 illustrates the creative process as it unfolds, as well as the layers within each human being, in which fire represents our spirit, air our mental processes, water our feelings and emotions, and Earth our physical body. In this version of the map, the point at the centre represents our soul, which is our Divine spark, where we are connected to the source of all life – which some people call God.

Having this spark of God within us allows us to be 'subcreators', as Tolkien put it. The processes we go through in order to create anything are identical to processes going on throughout creation. They work best when we 'co-create', with the rest of humanity and with the invisible powers in creation.

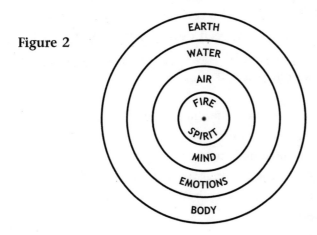

Figure 2

Course Activities

The structure of the course is designed to help you get back in touch with your own initial impulse (Part 1 – Fire) and with your soul's creative plan, or code (Part 2 – Air). When you have reclaimed that code, you will understand how to nurture it (Part 3 – Water), and you will be able to make a plan of action (Part 4 – Earth), to take you forward.

Between each of these four parts, I have included some 'interludes'. These are intended to set you thinking about various topics, such as our relationship to time and the amount of freedom we have. Thinking about these issues will help you reconsider how you live in the world and will support your new way of thinking about your choices – the choices that shape your destiny.

Each week you will need to set aside about three hours for an intensive session, outlined below. You will also need some time during the week to carry out various tasks and activities, some of which may consist of just thinking about certain aspects of your life, which can often be done while you are on a journey, or while you are gardening, when your mind can drift for a while (but not while driving).

Your Weekly Session

Make this a regular afternoon or evening when you will not be disturbed. Let friends and family know that this is your sacred time and switch off the phone. I recommend evenings for your sessions. If you go to sleep shortly after a session, your dream life will take up on any themes you have been dealing with, and you may get helpful messages – without trying!

During your session you will:

❖ Meditate and talk to your guardian angel.
❖ Write in your journal (see below), recording any insights and inspirations you have had since the previous week.
❖ Read your tasks for the coming week. Do those that can be done immediately and plan any activities that have to be fitted in during the week.

Ongoing Activities

Each week I shall be outlining a set of specific tasks for the next stage of your journey. Some are designed to be included in your weekly sessions, others you will need to think about or act upon during the week, including spending some time doing some personal research. There are also a number of activities that you need to carry out regularly throughout the course:

KEEPING A JOURNAL

Your journal is for recording conversations with your guardian angel; for writing your insights and for accounts of any inspiring events. Make it special: buy a beautiful unlined notebook, or buy a plain book and design your personal cover for it. Always use plain paper, so that you can write in different directions, draw pictures or add coloured symbols or postcards and photographs.

RESEARCH

This will include exploring your family background, perhaps by using the Internet or your local library.

KEEPING A NOTEBOOK

Keep a notebook by you all the time, so that you can scribble down notes and insights to transfer later into your journal.

RECORDING YOUR DREAMS

Keep your notebook and a pen by your bed for noting down dreams as soon as you wake. As you go to sleep each night you can ask your guardian angel to help you in your process by allowing useful dreams to emerge. Later, you can add any important dreams to your special journal.

MUSING

The time between sessions will bear more fruit if you allow some time for musing or daydreaming. Musing allows unexpected insights to bubble up to the surface of the mind. You can relax in an armchair, or let your mind wander while you are gardening or washing up, but the ideal activity for this is walking; the rhythmical movements of the body seem to encourage clear and creative thinking. If you can, go for a walk at least once a week, perhaps just before your weekly session, keeping your notebook with you to note down unexpected insights.

CREATING COLLAGES AND LIFE 'MAPS'

Get in a good stock of coloured pens, pencils, pastels – whatever you like working with. As well as your journal you will need some large sheets of drawing paper (size A1 or 594x841mm); you will also find a roll of lining paper useful for creating things like family trees. Have some glue for making collages, and any bits and pieces, such as shiny or coloured papers, star stickers and so on, which will help create pictures – no artistic experience needed.

KEEPING A TREASURE FOLDER OR BOX FILE

This is to store cuttings, photographs, pictures from magazines, inspiring poems and your own creations. Again, choose something special, or take a plain box or folder and decorate it.

There is quite a lot to do and the amount of time you have available may vary throughout the course – you may not cover every single activity and exercise each week. Don't put yourself under pressure but work according to your own situation and at your own pace. You may wish to take longer than 12 weeks but beware of losing the thread if you take too long. Equally, I recommend that you do not try to hurry through the process.

Constant Help from Your Guardian Angel

The essential first step before beginning the course is to establish or re-establish your connection with your guardian angel. A few days before you start your first weekly session, take yourself through the visualisation below. I use it in my workshops and it is included in my book *Living with Angels* (Piatkus, 2003). Make sure you pick a time when you will not be disturbed.

If you have read *Living with Angels* and are already familiar with the visualisation, you may find this process unnecessary. If so, you should still spend some time in your sacred space talking to your guardian angel, in order to make sure your connection is strong. Tell him or her that you are planning to do this course; you will be checking in once a week for a session and that you would also like extra special help between sessions to complete your tasks.

You may wish to tape-record the visualisation in advance, rather than trying to remember the instructions.

A Journey to Meet Your Guardian Angel

Give yourself plenty of time, and before you start, create a beautiful and peaceful environment for yourself. If you wish, you could light a candle or burn some incense. Make sure you will not be disturbed – take the phone off the hook.

❖ Observe your breathing, allowing it to settle into a gentle rhythm. Breathe deeply, breathe slowly.
❖ Imagine you are in a beautiful sitting room. You are sitting on a comfortable sofa, facing glass doors which open on to a wonderful garden. In your mind's eye, you rise from the sofa and walk over to the doors. You open them carefully and step out into the garden.
❖ You wander through the garden where the colours of the flowers and the dewy grass seem brighter than anything you have ever seen. You can smell the perfume of the flowers and the newly mown grass. You can see butterflies flitting among the blossoms. You can hear birds singing in the clear blue sky above you.
❖ As you walk slowly through the garden you come to a gate, which leads out of the garden. You open the gate and find yourself in a country lane.
❖ You walk along the lane. On one side is a hedge full of birds and little animals. On the other is a field of corn, with brightly coloured wild flowers – poppies, daisies and cornflowers.
❖ Eventually you come to some trees and find yourself wandering

23

into a wood. The wood is quiet and you notice how the sun shimmers through the green and golden leaves.

❖ There is a path through the wood, marked with shining white stones. Although the trees are getting thicker, there seems to be a light ahead of you and you keep following the white stones until you come to a clearing, where the light comes from.

❖ In the clearing you find a shining building and you know that this is a sacred space which has been waiting for you.

❖ The door of your sacred building is open and you sense that a welcome awaits you. As you walk inside you know that you have come home. The door gently closes behind you, to provide a safe haven.

❖ You find yourself in a golden room with a seat waiting for you. When you sit down you feel peaceful, happy and content. This is the place where you will meet and talk to your guardian angel.

❖ Ask in your mind: 'I now call my guardian angel to come to me. I would like to know your name and please tell me anything I need to know which is important to me at this stage on my life path.'

❖ *Allow about three minutes' silence at this point, so that you can talk to your guardian angel.*

❖ Now say thank you to your guardian angel and get up from your seat. Move gently towards the door of your sacred room.

❖ You can still feel the presence of your guardian angel. As the doors open gently you step outside and start moving down the path of white stones which guides you through the wood.

❖ Gradually the trees begin to thin out and you can see the sun shining through the leaves.

❖ You find yourself back on the path through the country. The hedge with birds and wild animals is on one side of you. The swaying golden corn and the wild flowers, scarlet poppies, white daisies and bright blue cornflowers are on the other.

❖ Eventually you find the gate which leads back into the garden, and you wander through the garden, smelling the flowers, and listening to the birds singing and the bees humming.

❖ You walk towards the house and step back through the open glass doors into the sitting room.

❖ Walk back to the comfortable sofa and sit down once more.

❖ Before opening your eyes, breathe deeply and stretch your body like a cat. Shrug your shoulders and wriggle your hands and feet.

❖ You may need to take some time before you open your eyes. When you do, remember to look down at the floor first. Coming back into everyday reality should be a gentle process.

Now take your time to write down your experience and draw an image if you wish. The process of writing sometimes brings more insight.

If you still feel slightly spaced out after writing, stand up and walk around, feeling your feet firmly on the floor. Eating a snack, or sipping some spring water, will also help to ground you. Or use the Sky, Roots, Sunshine exercise on page 31.

Your Experience

Whatever you experienced is right for you. There are as many different guardian angels as there are people. And there are an equal number of individual experiences. Some people visualise clearly, others receive more of an impression. When they arrive in the clearing in the wood, some people find a splendid temple like the Taj Mahal awaiting them, some find a simple chapel or a wooden hut, such as a hermit might use. Grand or simple, this is a powerful space for you, chosen by a deep part of yourself as a suitable place to retreat to when you need answers to life's problems. You can go back to this space in your mind at any time. Use it as your inner, holy sanctuary.

Your guardian angel, too, may arrive in one of many different guises. You may see nothing, but simply feel a presence beside you, or just behind you. You may have an impression of a shadowy figure, or of a bright light. Sometimes people do see an angel with wings but more often there is a sensation, accompanied by light and a feeling of joyfulness.

Not everyone gets a response first time to the request for a name.

And this is fine – the name will come to you when it is important. One young woman on a workshop actually heard the name spoken in her ear – which made her jump – but this is fairly unusual. And one of my students, who described the sensation of a silvery-blue presence, heard the name 'Alariel' as 'a high, fine sound, like a light breeze or a breath of sound'. Some people are given ordinary names like Tom or Jane, and that is also fine. Your guardian angel is a companionable sort of being and will give you a name that is comfortable for you. Do trust this process. If he says his name is Tom, then use the name Tom when you call him. If you don't get a name, trust this as well – one of my home study students told me that her guardian angel explained that she was actually not allowed to know their name, as it would provide a distraction.

Over the next 12 weeks your personal connection with your guardian angel will develop and become richer – rather like becoming more intimate with a human partner as your relationship grows. And, like a human relationship, the bond becomes stronger as you honour the presence of the other in your life. Be devoted to your quest and highly focused on your new journey and your guardian angel will respond with plenty of signs and messages, through other people, surprising events, magical opportunities and dreams.

Preparing for Your Weekly Session

This section is essential reading. It explains how to create a good working structure and provides you with tools for protecting and nurturing yourself while you are doing deep inner work.

First of all, please honour the process of this course by allowing yourself the time that you need and keeping it for yourself religiously. Time is an essential ingredient in the incarnation process and we need to have a positive relationship with Old Father Time. If we try to rush the process in our impatience for results, then our vision will be only a partial reality; on the other hand, if we procrastinate, nothing will happen at all. So make a commitment to put in the time for your research, note-taking and musing. For your weekly session, one three-hour slot will be sufficient. Even a small peek into the hidden realms of the soul and the guardian angel are bound to bring up an enormous wealth of material which will need time to process. But your commitment will reap rich rewards.

While not essential, it would be helpful to find a friend, preferably someone who would like to do the course with you, or at least a friend who would be happy to hear what you are doing and offer a sympathetic ear when you want to talk about what comes up. Incidentally, the work you will be doing is not intended to replace therapy but to give you a new way of looking at your life, which I believe can only have positive results. However, if you have had any serious emotional difficulties in your past, I would recommend that you first discuss the course with a counsellor who can advise you on whether the material is suitable for you personally.

It is also important not to use any mind-bending drugs during this course, and this includes excessive quantities of alcohol: you need to be particular about your psychic and psychological boundaries while doing this work.

Before you embark on your first week, please read the list of recommendations below, which will support you while you are working at a deep level.

Recommendations

CHOOSE A BUDDY

Ask a friend to be your buddy or confidant(e). It would be ideal if he or she would like to work through the course with you but, if this is not possible, ask a trusted friend to support you once a week. You can either meet in person or, if he or she is at a distance, arrange to telephone each other. A face-to-face meeting is better than a phone call but, either way, make this as soon as possible after your weekly session.

If you are both working on the course, take it in turns to listen to each other and give any feedback you feel appropriate. If you are working by telephone, I suggest you make two separate calls, one when you talk to your friend about your experience, and one when you act as listener.

PREPARE YOUR ENVIRONMENT

Create a sacred space for yourself, using candles, incense and any other props you find significant, such as pictures, crystals, stones and other natural objects. If you cannot leave these in place between sessions, find a beautiful box to keep them in. Wrap each item in some special fabric, such as a brightly coloured piece of silk, and make a ritual of the process of unpacking and packing them each time. (There is a list of helpful crystals in Appendix 3 on page 217.)

Look in your CD collection for music that inspires you but also keeps you in a calm and relaxed mood – though not so relaxing that it sends you to sleep. Keep a good selection handy for your session. Music is very much a matter of personal choice but I find that music played on instruments, rather than synthesised, speaks more directly to the soul. The lute and the flute are excellent – both are associated with angels and spiritual realms.

PREPARE YOURSELF

Open your weekly session by asking the angels and higher powers to protect your personal boundaries and your sacred space. You may wish to use the Invocation to the Four Archangels or the Power Pentagram (see pages 29–31).

During your sessions, you may experience anger and sadness, as well as joy and sudden flashes of insight. So keep a box of tissues by you, just in case there are tears, and a bottle of Rescue Remedy. If you do experience intense emotions, you may find it helpful to use other Bach Flower Remedies for specific emotional states. (Some are suggested in Appendix 3 on page 216.)

COMPLETING YOUR SESSIONS

Immediately after your session, pack away your journal and any other work you have been doing in your treasure file or box. Blow out any candles with a blessing to the world. Then make sure that you are fully grounded. You could use a grounding exercise such as the Sky, Roots, Sunshine exercise (page 31). Or, depending on the time of day, you could take some other kind of exercise – yoga, dancing, walking or cycling are all good. You will have shifted a lot of psychic energy, so any lively physical activity, such as a good walk or an up-tempo dance around your sitting room, will move the energy around your physical system. Afterwards, you could take a bath, using aromatherapy oils. Suitable oils are suggested in Appendix 3 page 216.

Opening and Closing, Protecting and Grounding

Deep investigations into the psyche create openings and soften the edges of the self, thus making us more vulnerable to emotional issues in other people. The search into our memories, which is part of the course and part of the inward quest for meaning, can be likened to deep-sea diving. We are plunging into the ocean of consciousness, hoping to collect the pearls and gems on the seabed. On the way down we may bump into pretty fishes, sweet starfishes – and occasionally, sea monsters. Some of these denizens of the deep may not belong to us; they may arise because we stray into the waters of the collective consciousness. Like divers, we need to equip ourselves with protective apparatus before we leap, and afterwards we need to bath, rest and recuperate. This is why it is vital to 'close down' after a session and to ground yourself back into your everyday being by using any of the methods just described.

---

1. INVOCATION TO THE FOUR ARCHANGELS

Once you are comfortable working with you guardian angel, you may like to start your sessions by invoking the four great archangels. Their presence provides powerful protective energy that can be called on whenever you use a room for sacred purposes. Open your invocation by using incense or a smudging stick, moving around the room anti-clockwise and stopping at points to indicate all four directions, north, east, south and west. At each point, speak the invocation aloud.

I summon Michael, archangel of the south, protector of fire.
I summon Gabriel, archangel of the west, protector of air.
I summon Auriel, archangel of the north, protector of earth.

I summon Raphael, archangel of the east, protector of water. Mighty archangels, guardians of the invisible kingdom, open the gates of light so that my spiritual work will benefit from your protection and power.

2. THE POWER PENTAGRAM FOR PROTECTION

The pentagram is often associated with magic, more especially 'magick', the kind of manipulative art practised by black magicians or witches. Of course, any powerful tool can be misused. But the pentagram is actually a grounding and essentially benevolent symbol, representing as it does the four elements – fire, earth, air and water – plus a fifth, described in medieval times as the *Quinta Essentia*, or the *Anima Mundi*, which is similar to *chi* or *prana*, the energy that pervades all life.

For this exercise, you need a pointer of some kind – an elegant paper knife would be suitable. Or just use the first finger of your right hand. Trace a pentagram in the air in front of you: bring your outstretched arm to the left side, at a point near the middle of your thigh. Move your arm upwards to a point corresponding to the top of your head. Then bring it down, to the point around the middle of the right thigh. By now you will have created an upside-down V shape in front of you. Now move your pointer upwards to a point slightly above your left shoulder, then carry it across, in a straight line, to the opposite point just above the right shoulder and then, in a diagonal to the point from which you started.

Figure 3

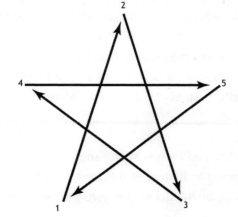

A single pentagram traced in the air is powerful protection or you can create a pentagram in each of the four directions and call on the archangels of the south, west, north and east at the same time.

3. SKY, ROOTS, SUNSHINE

When you have finished a session a simple grounding exercise is to imagine yourself as a tree. Stand up straight, raise your arms and stretch them above your head, saying, 'I reach for the blue sky.' Then drop down from the waist and (if possible) touch the floor, saying, 'I grow down into the brown earth.' As you do so, imagine roots growing from your feet into the ground beneath. Come back up to standing position and bring your arms around in a curve, as if hugging a large balloon, and say, 'I gather the golden sunshine into my being.' Then hug yourself. Needless to say, getting into real, physical contact with nature is the most grounding thing anyone can do.

Once you have met your guardian angel and made your preparations, you will be ready to embark on Part 1 of the course. Make sure that you are familiar with the contents of this chapter first and refer back to it if necessary.

Now you can really get started. If you haven't already done so, make a date with yourself for your first weekly session when you will read the next section, on fire, and the material for Week 1.

Good luck with your journey – I hope you will find it exciting and inspiring.

PART 1

The World of
Creative Intention – Fire

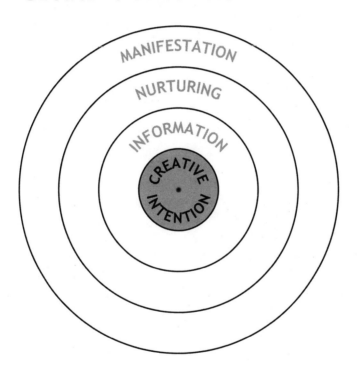

The World of Creative Intention – Fire

Life is a pure flame, and we live by an invisible sun within us.
SIR THOMAS BROWNE

To achieve anything in life, we need to start with a clear intention, fired by enthusiasm. This creative impulse, which drives everything, is symbolised by the element of fire. In order to start creating a life that you love and fulfilling your own destiny, you first need to identify the deep passions in your heart – everybody has them, even people who don't appear to be passionate about anything. During the first stage of your journey, you will be uncovering the true desires of your own soul, that initial spark that you may have lost touch with. You will be looking for the clues that will remind you: 'So that's who I wanted to be before I was born.'

> FIRE is active, dynamic, fascinating and dangerous. Throughout man's history, fire has been a potent force, with its capacity to nurture life – through its warmth and its ability to transform food – and to take it violently away. In all the ancient religions it was seen as a symbol of Divine power. There are many references to it in the Bible: Moses found God speaking from a burning bush; a seraph touched the prophet Isaiah on the lips with a hot coal, enabling him to speak with Divine inspiration. The disciples of Jesus were touched with a Divine flame at the feast of Pentecost, signifying their mission to preach the gospel.

In classical mythology, the Titan Prometheus stole fire from the gods and gave it to primitive mortals, who had been living in dark caves, with the result that they developed all kinds of creative gifts. (Prometheus was cruelly punished for his audacity, bound to a rock where an eagle tore out his liver daily until he was finally released by Hercules.) The Roman god Vulcan was the god of fire as well as a blacksmith who forged thunderbolts.

In Ancient Rome, a fire was kept permanently lit in the temple of Vesta, a living symbol of the power of the state, guarded by the Vestal Virgins. Synagogues, churches and temples usually have a lamp constantly burning, to represent the Divine presence and, in the Zoroastrian religion, every household possesses the sacred fire, which has immense spiritual importance.

Love, both spiritual and personal, has often been likened by mystics and poets to a flame in the heart. And when we think about people who are generous, or enthusiastic, we often describe them as 'warm-hearted' or 'fiery'.

Sometimes fire is used to represent a spiritual ordeal, just as gold is refined by passing through fire, and steel is tempered in fire. Spiritual teachers emphasise that we may have trials and tribulations on our life's journey that may be a bit too hot for comfort. In Mozart's wonderful opera *The Magic Flute* (which draws on Masonic teachings), the young lovers have to go through an ordeal by fire and water before they reach their goal.

Within ourselves there is an inner fire that desires to bring beauty, truth and joy into the world. In order to fulfil our potential, we need to be in touch with this fire – our creative willpower. When we first came into the world and during the early stages of our life, this power was intense and alive. Then as we grew older, external influences – family, culture and social forces – all too often dampened that flame, turning us away from our original pure intention.

The first influence in our lives is our parents, who in turn carry influences from many previous generations. We all arrive with our own soul's code and whether we can easily follow this through and manifest it depends a great deal on the circumstances we encounter in our childhood. This is why it is so helpful to look at the family we arrived into, the local and national culture, and any spiritual or religious influences on our early lives. You may have been adopted into it, or conceived by artificial means, but it is still your family of choice. In the past, unwanted babies were frequently left on doorsteps, or taken into monastic institutions. Some of these children turned out to be the more interesting characters in history.

One of my students told the group that she felt that when she arrived in the world everything was wonderful: she likened it to finding herself in a beautiful swimming pool, filled with clear blue water. Then, she said, she felt as though rubbish had been thrown into her pool, so that she could not swim freely any more. I asked her who or what had spoilt her freedom to swim and she made a long list of people, including family and schoolteachers, whom she felt had dumped rubbish into her life that she didn't know how to deal with. We invented a special visualisation for her, in which several helpful people she had met later in life threw her a swimming ring to give her new confidence.

During this first stage of the course, you will be researching your own story. What kind of family brought you into the world? Who supported and who sabotaged your soul's code? What events can you identify that demonstrate the presence of your guardian angel along the way? I have noticed that it is often people like aunts, uncles and grandparents, or even a neighbour in the street, who bring a growing child a message that stirs their passion, perhaps in the shape of a book or a present. When I was nine years old one of my aunts sent me a birthday card with a picture of a lamb on it. Inside she wrote: 'You really are a little lamb – ask your mother.' My mother explained that this was because I was born under the sign of Aries. This was the spark that first awakened my latent interest in astrology. (Later, I had a past-life regression in which I recalled being the son of an astrologer in ancient Babylon.)

Although my stepfather was sceptical, and my mother did not know as much about astrology as my aunt, we did have a book on the subject in the house, published by the Theosophical Society, and through this I started learning about esoteric wisdom. Most people would say that I had been influenced by this event. But I strongly believe that no one influences a soul's choice; rather the soul calls out for what it needs. If my path had not been to study esoteric wisdom, the birthday card would not have struck a chord in my soul.

So, during the first stage of your journey, you will be asked to identify the people and events in your early life that gave you clues to the song your soul wants to sing. It is true that people's opinions and attitudes can discourage you from listening to your soul needs and you will also be looking for any signs that this happened to you. You will be working with your guardian angel, to reach your soul's code and awaken your dormant passions and desires. This is a time when you can fan your inner fire and bring it up to a fine blaze.

During Weeks 1 and 2 you will be doing some research into your family and personal history, in order to catch a glimpse of yourself in the early stages of this incarnation. You will probably need to speak to some of your relations in order to retrieve background information. A lot of this may come quite easily to you, though sometimes questions can cause uncomfortable ripples. Many of your relatives may be happy to natter on about how wonderful or terrible you were as a toddler or teenager. But some family closets contain skeletons and you may draw some blanks. Don't get frustrated if your family history takes time to unravel; the information that is important to you will come to you one way or another. Also, although it would be neat to collect your story chronologically, you are bound to find that clues crop up in no particular order. For, example, you may be asking your aunt about your great-grandmother for Week 1's research, when she starts telling you about something that happened when you were four. Note down anything that seems relevant in your notebook and come back to it later.

If you are adopted, or for some other reason are not in touch with your biological parents, it's important to realise that the family you are with now is the family that was chosen by your soul for this incarnation. Your biological parents created the means for you to find them.

While you are sifting through old family material and stories of your youth, you may find that memories and dreams occur that provide additional insights. Keep a note of these in your journal, where you will be building up a collage of stories, memories, images, all of which help to create a picture of your soul's code. If you are committed to uncovering your inner blueprint, there are many ways in which the information can arrive. Be prepared for surprises, synchronicities and even miracles.

Week 1

Your Start in Life

*Who shows a child as he really is? Who sets him in his
constellation and puts the measuring rod in his hand?*
RAINER MARIA RILKE

This week's aim is to get a picture of your family, your ancestry –
for better or worse – and some of its history. Before we are born,
we choose the most appropriate scenario we can find, in order to
carry through our spiritual intentions. In Weeks 2 and 3 you will
be finding out more about your soul's code and how to reconnect
with it. But the family we have chosen to be born into gives us the
first set of clues we need for uncovering why we have come into
this particular life, at this particular time. So I am going to suggest
a series of tasks that will help you identify the effects of your being
a member of your particular family.

You will be asking yourself some searching questions: how has
being in your family affected you? Has your family background
taken you away from your true path, or made you more determined
to follow it? Looking at these issues is all part of your road to self-
knowledge and self-development. If you have never felt quite 'at
home' with your parents, siblings and other relatives, you may
wonder why you have chosen such an unsuitable family. Remember
that the choice has been made by your soul for particular reasons
and this work should help you to discover what they were.

Your family and culture could be described as the soil in which your little acorn, your soul's code, has chosen to grow. You may remember Jesus' parable of the farmer sowing seeds: some seeds fail to flourish because they fall upon 'stony ground'. Some people I work with definitely feel that their families obstructed their growth and it is true that many people take a long time to come into their own – sadly, some never really succeed. But don't forget that some plants actually thrive on stony ground: the oldest plant in the world, the Methuselah Tree, which is nearly 5,000 years old, grows on a windswept mountain in California. All living things, including humans, are extremely adaptable and sometimes too much comfort can reduce motivation. It is up to each human being to use their circumstances to their best advantage; your guardian angel can help you connect with higher powers to shift the balance in your favour, putting you in touch with resources that go beyond immediate family and culture.

What I want you to do this week is to take a close look at your social and family background and identify the advantages and disadvantages that came with it. Perhaps my own story will help here. My father was born into a family of devout Roman Catholics but he rejected conventional Christianity to tread a rather eccentric spiritual path of his own. I did not know any of this when I was a child. My parents had divorced and I had no contact with my father's family, who lived in Canada. My stepfather and my mother were Socialists, not at all religious, and the only contact I had with religion was through my local Church of England primary school. Yet, whenever the school took us to church for Harvest Festivals, or at Christmas and Easter, I was entranced. I asked to go to Sunday School, much to my family's amusement and created an altar in my bedroom – more amusement.

For a naturally religious child to be surrounded by sceptics could be seen as a grave disadvantage. I was told that religion caused more problems for humans than it solved. However, because I had plenty of intellectual freedom, no one stopped me reading about world religions or esoteric subjects, like astrology and the chakras. The Catholic family in Canada would not have given me that privilege.

So you can see that the desire for spirituality, which I was born

41

with, was supported, even though the ground looked a bit stony. It is also worth mentioning here that my mother, in calling me Theolyn, gave me exactly the right kind of name for the path I would lead. 'Theo' means 'God' and 'lyn' means a river or a stream. The name you are given is always significant.

The Vale of Soul Making

The poet John Keats referred to the world as the 'vale of soul-making'. This is a perfect description of the process by which the soul uses its time on Earth to learn about its own nature and to grow in depth and beauty. Each of us has a particular role to play in the development of the collective soul of humanity, so the quality of our individual lives is crucial to the happiness of the whole. Every incarnation on Earth provides a new opportunity to expand the experience of the soul, so that we become more compassionate, more inclusive and more able to use the power of the life force wisely.

As you will see, your main task this week will be finding out about your family and its background. Perhaps you come from a family that is already interested in its history and has kept lots of records. However, I suspect that most of you will get just a handful of stories and possibly a few photographs. The family story may be quite misty. Don't worry about this; I am not training you as a genealogist. Whatever you need to know will arrive. And, please be aware of the Chinese Whispers factor – family stories repeated over time have a habit of being enhanced, or possibly played down, but usually altered.

What counts here is the story, the inner truth, not necessarily the bare facts. Obviously, none of us will ever be entirely free from the culture we were born into, but the choice your soul made to arrive in a European or American family, rather than, say, an Inuit tribe, is also relevant to your quest. And it is also possible that the call of your soul will have taken you from one social group or country to another.

Simon's Story

Here is a great tale about a family mystery which illustrates how opinions about the truth can differ.

Simon is one of three brothers born in the Midlands. The family had been working class for several generations but Simon's parents had improved their status, especially as his mother had become a teacher and had risen to deputy head. The three boys were notable in the local schools for being exceptionally brainy. Simon recalls getting into trouble at five years old when he pointed out to his class teacher that spiders were not insects. When, next day, he took in a book to prove his point, he was in even more trouble. Simon's two brothers went to Oxford University but Simon employs his own brilliance in the visual arts and as a musician. His father was also gifted with words, music and art, even though he had not been able to finish at art school and had rather an uninspiring job.

Simon's aunt (his father's sister) told him a story which she felt explained why there was so much cleverness around. The boys' great-grandfather was the illegitimate son of a girl who had been in service at a manor house. When she became pregnant, the girl left her job and married a local man who gave his surname to her son. She had other children by her husband but only the illegitimate one was bookish and clever. Simon's aunt was quite convinced that the serving girl had become pregnant by a member of the local aristocracy and that the child's blue blood had brought with it an appreciation of the finer things in life, as well as intellectual gifts. She felt this story was substantiated by the fact that the baby had been given, as his first name, the family name of some local gentry.

Simon's father had a quite different version. Being a democratic man, he believed that nurture, not nature, was the source of intelligence. He pointed out that being aristocratic does not necessarily supply you with brainpower – often, quite the reverse. And, he claimed, appreciation of the arts and musical gifts are learned rather than inherited. His favourite contender for the stranger who bedded his grandmother was a Scots Guardsman (it was known that the Guards had been billeted locally at the time). As several members of the family had a distinctively Celtic look, with reddish hair and beards, this also seemed plausible.

We can see from this story that members of a family will choose a version of a story that suits their own belief system. Simon was quite happy with the aristocratic version. The story also highlights an important issue for your own quest. It reminds us of the question of 'nature or nurture'. Most modern psychologists will agree that we are a subtle blend of both. Investigations into the lives of identical twins separated at birth suggest that they have all kinds of characteristics in common that previously might have been thought of as learned behaviour, influenced by people around them, such as their choice of colours, or food or religion. One of my daughters has an intense dislike of bananas and she certainly didn't learn that from her dad, who loves them. But her grandfather has the same intense reaction when you even mention the word. These kinds of similarities suggest that we inherit more than our physical characteristics through our genes.

I prefer to step aside from the nature versus nurture argument; I believe that whatever our genetic inheritance and whatever the family context, good or bad, we have the freedom to make fundamental choices about what we do, what we become and how we behave. Whoever his great-grandfather was, Simon himself brought his gifts into this life. And any constraints that seem to inhibit our progress are to do with how we think about ourselves. Even physical disabilities or shortfalls can be overcome if the will is strong. If anyone ever told Wayne Sleep that he wasn't tall enough to become a top male ballet dancer, it seems that he didn't listen. Wayne, only five feet tall, is one of the best known and best loved English dancers and a great creative choreographer. People with no legs have become great athletes; women in their eighties go up the Amazon in primitive canoes. Most limiting factors are in the mind.

This Week's Session

❖ Switch off the phone and arrange your space, collecting any beautiful things and music you want around you. Light a candle and some incense if you wish.

❖ Use your preferred technique for starting your session.

❖ Now sit comfortably, relax, close your eyes and visualise yourself going to the sacred building where you met your guardian angel. You will be visiting this magical place each week, as a rendezvous for your inner meeting with your guardian angel. See yourself sitting inside this building, as you did before. Then ask inwardly:

Dear guardian angel [use his or her name if you have been given one], I am working to discover my soul's code for this lifetime; please help me in this process and guide me as I search for memories and clues. My aim this week is to find out about the family I came into and to recall the reasons for my choice. If there is anything that will help me at this stage, please let me know, either now, or in my dreams.

❖ Now sit quietly for a few moments, giving time for your guardian angel to respond. Then gently come out of your meditation and if you have received a response, write it down in your journal. Sometimes responses may come later, in the form of a dream or a flash of insight.

Tasks for this Session

❖ In your notebook write down some notes, describing what you think was going on when you were born. Include your full name, the date and the place of your birth, your parents' situation and a general impression of the first six months of your life. For example: '20 August 1970: Janet Mary to Jimmy Grantham and Marjorie Smith, Oxfordshire. Jimmy had been barracked at Brize Norton with the US Airforce, said he would marry Marjorie and take her back to the States. He went home on leave before Janet was born and was never heard of again. Marjorie went to Derbyshire and stayed with her aunt, always expecting Jimmy would come back. Mum had to help with making beds in her aunt's bed and breakfast . . .'

❖ On a large sheet of paper, draw up a family tree, going back as far as your great-grandparents. Don't worry if there are some gaps; treat this as a basic outline. During the coming week you will be collecting more information. All you need for now is names and, if you have them, dates.

❖ In your notebook, writing as quickly as you can so that you don't think too hard about your responses, make a list of as many people whom you know were around you when you were a small baby: aunts, uncles, grandparents, brothers and sisters, neighbours – anyone who came into contact with you during the first three years of your life. As you write their names put a plus sign or minus sign beside each one, to indicate whether this person had a helpful or hindering effect. Don't reason about this, just put down your overall gut feeling.

❖ Now think about the most significant people on that list and identify what their importance was in your early life, whether supportive or not. You might want to include someone who was missing – they could still have been significant. Jimmy Grantham's disappearance, in the example above, would have had a profound effect on Janet's life. In your notebook, write beside each name the probable reason for choosing them to be in your life.

❖ Finally, read the following suggestions for your tasks during the coming week. Make a list in your notebook, with reminders of anyone you need to contact, or any places you may wish to visit.

Tasks for the Week

During the coming week you will start researching your family background. Don't expect to complete it all in one week; once you've set the ball rolling you will probably gather more information throughout the course and you may find yourself sufficiently interested to take plenty of time over it.

Below you will find a list of suggestions for gleaning an impression of the family you have chosen for this incarnation. You obviously will not be able to cover them all but they are designed to get you going. Use your intuition and follow the trail that seems to call to you. Human history is a glorious fabric woven from many threads over generations and, as you go on, you will get glimpses into the section of that great tapestry that is most significant for you. As you collect your family information, write it in your journal and illustrate it with any relevant photographs, old letters, or other mementoes you may come across.

Think of yourself as a Sherlock Holmes, looking for clues and also mulling things over. Although renowned for his crisp logic, the great fictional detective recognised that the mind needs to get into a relaxed state in order to get the best results. If he had a tricky case he would call it a 'three-pipe problem' – that is, he needed to sit, musing and smoking, until the answer came to him. You will often find that answers, or pieces of information, simply arrive when you stop trying too hard. Once you have your mind on the case, you will find synchronicities cropping up all the time. For instance, family members may well hear of your quest and ring you up out of the blue with a story to tell.

Another lesson you can learn from Sherlock Holmes is to stand slightly apart from your findings. Obviously, if you uncover some tragic story you will have an emotional reaction and I do not want you to deny or reject those feelings. But part of this process is to begin to see your own life and the lives of your ancestors as chapters in an unfolding story and not to get caught up in judgements about whether someone was 'right' or 'wrong', or whether some event was 'good' or 'bad'. Family stories will always be coloured by people's opinions: the young man who left his home town to escape an overbearing father may be criticised by his remaining siblings but he may have initiated a train of events elsewhere that are beneficial for people the family know nothing about. Finally, remember that people will report what they personally find interesting and may have chosen to recall a particular part of a story that resonates with their own soul's journey. And, as in Simon's story, they are likely to interpret events, or even add colour, according to their own likes and dislikes.

As part of your week's work, contact your chosen buddy, if you have one. Discussing your discoveries with someone else may throw new light on them.

Suggestions for Your Family Research

❖ Ask yourself what kind of family you came into, whether you were born into it or adopted. Were they rich, poor, intellectual, artistic, uneducated? How did this affect your own needs and desires? Did one side of the family show a marked contrast with the other?

❖ Collect as many family stories about past generations as you can. Often families have favourite stories that you may have heard repeated at family gatherings. Equally, there may be older relatives still living who will give you some totally new information.

❖ Use the Internet to discover the history of your family names. Did anyone adopt a new name at any time? What does your own first name mean? Were you named after anyone in the family?

❖ As well as people's names, identify the places they came from. Track anyone who came from a foreign country, perhaps as a refugee, or in order to create a better life, or perhaps fleeing from the law, or as a deportee.

❖ Were any of your ancestors caught up in significant events – the French Revolution, the pogroms in Russia and Germany, the voyage of the Pilgrim Fathers? Were there any events that changed everything, for better or worse? Are there any mysteries to be solved?

❖ Was your family well grounded and stable? Or did they struggle to survive? How did this affect you?

❖ Did your parents have great aspirations for you, urging you on to improve yourself? Was this an advantage, or a restriction?

❖ Did your family have a sense of tradition, so that you often heard stories about earlier generations?

❖ Have you inherited any talents or gifts that have already appeared or perhaps have lain dormant in previous generations? Your father may have been keen on amateur dramatics and you may have taken this further by going into the theatre yourself. Or this dramatic talent may have skipped a generation, because one of your great-grandparents prevented their children from going into such an 'undesirable' profession.

Summary

Nowadays the Internet makes it much easier to track earlier generations or people with your family name. This course is not about genealogy but it is useful to get an idea of the human inheritance you have chosen for this lifetime. If your family was rich or poor, if you had famous or infamous ancestors, if there was a strong professional line – a dynasty of doctors, lawyers or actors – any of these factors, and others too many to mention, will have created an atmosphere around you as a growing child. This atmosphere provided you with a background canvas against which your early years unfolded. When you can describe your family dispassionately, setting aside the emotional issues that are bound to colour your responses, then and only then can you make clear choices about your own destiny.

Families can go through enormous changes. During the Second World War, many Jewish people were forced to flee their homes; some changed their names and identities and kept the truth secret, even from their own children. Sometimes families emigrated across the sea to Australia or America in order to improve their lives, as my great-grandparents did. Sometimes people disappear after inter-family squabbles and cease communicating.

These hidden, often ancient, undercurrents have as much effect on young children as the things that are openly said or done. In the course of your investigations you may uncover old issues that at first seem to have nothing to do with you. Then you may come to realise that these stories have had a ripple effect through the generations. Often the outsiders and oddballs are the characters that can tell you the most important stuff. This is because the outsider in a family or tribe challenges the natural tendency of every group to feel safe by keeping things as they are. But the desire for safety and security often muffles or represses true creativity. The risk-takers in your family story have been trying to stretch the boundaries and create new possibilities.

Even if you feel your family background did not encourage your natural gifts and talents, there is still meaning to be found in this part of your story. Difficulties can provoke us to get ahead under our own steam – perhaps your soul chose these very difficulties in order to make you stronger. Getting in touch with any anger and frustration can take us back to our soul's real desires. During this course I will be encouraging you to view your life from a new angle, so that you get a fresh perspective – one that empowers you. *Your family is whatever it is – do not blame, do not complain.*

Blaming others, complaining about past events, or even trying to explain why things are the way they are – all these are admissions of your lack of power. They reduce your ability to take a powerful stand and take charge of your future. If you allow yourself to be a victim of circumstance, or of other people's attitudes and behaviour, you will not be able to see yourself stepping into a destiny that you have chosen for yourself. Even people who have been abused or neglected can come to realise that they need to let go of the pain and anger and establish a new way of thinking about their life, so that they can move on. Whatever family you have been born into, you now have the freedom to become what you want to be. Your family may have supported or thwarted you but, now that you are old enough to read this book, you are old enough to stand up and say I AM WHO I AM.

Don't forget, you can always turn to your guardian angel, who will help you see old difficulties and issues for what they really are – old. This course is all about clearing old clutter, the baggage that holds you back so that, as you proceed, you will find it easier and easier to see the old stories in a fresh light.

CLOSING DOWN

Now you have come to the end of your first session, with plenty of thoughts for what to do in the week before your second this time next week. Use your chosen methods for closing down and grounding yourself. And remember to thank your guardian angel.

Week 2

Your Heart's Desire

*Trying to remember myself as a child, I see something like
an outline drawing of the adult that I am now – funda-
mentally the same person but nothing filled in.*
DAME MARGOT FONTEYN

This week's aim is to recall what created a buzz of excitement for
you when you were small. Passion is a quality associated with fire.
Children feel passionately for and against things – clothes, school
subjects, games. What were your passions? And do they still play
a part in your life? You will also be researching what circumstances
supported or thwarted these passions. And – very important this –
you will be thinking about the name you were given, why it was
chosen and what it means.

So in this week's tasks, you will be taking a close look at your
childhood. Please note that this is not intended as a form of psycho-
analysis. If you find the tasks painful, please confide in your buddy
or, if necessary, talk to a counsellor. The purpose of the exercise is
to look for the clues that will put you back in touch with your original heart's desire. When you were little, your real gifts and talents
were ready to sprout and begin to flower. If for any reason they
were not well nurtured, you may have abandoned them or even
forgotten what they were.

It is said that 'the child is father to the man'. In other words,
when you were small everything that you could grow into was

already present, as an oak is present in an acorn. Even before a baby learns to speak it can demonstrate its innate talents. One of my children (the daughter who later went to ballet school) held on to the sofa before she could walk, using it as a barre and swinging her leg like a ballet dancer. The same little girl also sang recognisable tunes before she could talk and she is now a singer who writes her own songs. As children gradually acquire language, the ability to ask for what they need and want improves. This is one of the most important stages in development. If needs and wants are thwarted – perhaps because the parents are hard up or because they don't really appreciate the child's needs – then the growing child may give up, feeling that their gifts are not appreciated.

Do you know the story of *Matilda* by Roald Dahl? Matilda is a splendid role model for children whose parents don't encourage or appreciate their talents. She is a clever little girl who is really keen to read books but her parents, who are none too bright, continually mock her for doing so much reading. Fortunately, she is supported by the local librarian and is strong enough in her soul not to be downtrodden by her parents. Roald Dahl's books are full of children who have to contend with uncaring and even cruel adults. His characters are extreme, of course, but they are based on an element of truth. The scary schoolteacher in the film of *Matilda* reminded me alarmingly of one of the primary school teachers I used to have. I still shiver when I think of Miss Rolls, with her black hair, pulled into plaits and rolled into twin buns, and her constant criticisms.

Adults are often unkind to children, even if their weapons are only words. Mockery, sarcasm and criticism can damage a child's self-esteem almost as much as physical abuse. Although children need boundaries and should be encouraged to behave properly, especially in their relationships with other children, adults need to be aware that continually saying 'no' to a child's creative urges or interests is highly discouraging and may dampen the fire of natural passion in the child's heart. A young child can say 'I want to do that' and, as long as the adults don't forbid it, he or she will go off and do it. And if, at first, the child doesn't succeed, they will probably keep trying, unless someone else sidetracks or discourages them. The ability to achieve something is fuelled by intention and certainty, and certainty is the most important of these.

When he was a small child, the great ballet dancer Rudolf Nureyev lived in terrible poverty. Often he would have no food and would faint at school. When he was seven his mother decided to treat her children to a visit to the ballet on New Year's Eve. She only managed to get one ticket but set off nonetheless with her three children, hoping they might be able to buy black-market tickets. So many people were pushing at the theatre doors that they collapsed and everyone surged in. Rudolf Nureyev was about to see his first ballet. This world of magic and beauty, passion, elegance and joy left him speechless; in his own mind the great dancer started on his path of genius. He knew that he wanted to dance, even though his father beat him for wanting to do something so effeminate. The intention was there and somehow Nureyev managed to keep his certainty alive, to the eventual enchantment of audiences everywhere.

It is not possible to identify why some people are able to maintain certainty in the face of adversity but we hear of many geniuses who do exactly that. I am quite sure that it is not to do with the guardian angel being ineffectual. Everyone is treated fairly at a soul level, but perhaps some people do have a larger helping of determination and refuse to take no for an answer. Indeed, adversity can make people even more determined to succeed. Don't be tempted to think there is a great deal of difference between the average person and the 'genius'. 'Genius' is the Latin word for the guiding spirit, or guardian angel, and we all have one. We all have 'genius' – whether we use it or not is another matter. If you keep in touch with that inner guidance, your own genius will shine out. This course aims not only to help you maintain a connection with your guardian angel (your genius) but to encourage your determination to listen and act upon the guidance available to you and so fulfil your potential.

What's in a Name?

One of this week's tasks will be to research the meaning of your name and to find why you were given it. When you discover the meaning of your name you will discover a great deal about your soul's creative intention. The first part of my own name means 'god' and by 'coincidence' my parents met at Westminster Abbey, after a performance of Handel's *Messiah*. My mother was not at all religious and had gone to the abbey because Kathleen Ferrier was singing. But this significant meeting, and the name she gave me, are important pieces in my own jigsaw, suggesting that I would follow a spiritual path. We did not have a Bible in our house but I discovered 'The Song of Solomon' in a poetry book when I was nine years old and, at about the same time, I created my first sacred space in my bedroom – a small table covered with a purple cloth. This is a good example of the clues you can uncover that will help you identify the essential threads from which you are weaving the tapestry of your life.

Each name has its own sound vibration and meaning. About 20 years ago a good psychic and healer called Helga told me that people should really use their whole name, rather than a nickname or abbreviation. This is because your name is powerfully connected to your soul's code. If, after investigating its meaning, you then feel the name is not right for you, then change it. In the Jewish tradition, when someone is very ill and likely to die, it has been customary to change that person's name – even if they are unconscious. The idea is that the change of name will change the destiny of the person and may therefore prevent their death.

When I was small I was always called 'Theo' for short or, sometimes, just 'The'. After talking to Helga, I realised that I would feel much happier using the full version of my name. Partly because the 'lyn' part of the name is about flowing as in a stream, or river, and partly because it sounded more feminine. I was really tired of people telling me that Theo is a man's name.

Trisha's Story

One of my students got hold of a copy of the newspaper for the day she was born and told the group what a liberating effect it had on her. Trisha was very concerned about the world and its future. She had always assumed that in her own childhood things had been much better and safer. Reading papers dated nearly three decades ago made her realise that the state of the world was just as scary then as it is now – things are not actually going 'from bad to worse'. During the discussion, we agreed that this has been true throughout history. Even in Greek and Roman times, before the advent of today's media, there were soothsayers roaming the streets, calling 'Woe, woe! We are all doomed!'

Trisha was also aware that her parents (her father was a Christian minister) had brought her into a world that they probably found scary, which may have influenced the way they brought her up. Reading the old newspaper changed Trisha's attitude to time and allowed her to see that human life has always been a struggle. As an unmarried mother she is living in an era when attitudes to sexuality and marriage are more relaxed, which is 'good' from her point of view. But there are plenty of things going on that she sees as 'bad' – for example, the air pollution in the city where she lives, which may be affecting her little boy's lungs.

Human history describes our efforts to make life better but it seems to be a continuous case of swings and roundabouts – for example, we make technological improvements but these in turn may be detrimental to the planet. There has never been a 'golden age' when things were all 'good'. Inner freedom comes when we stand in the centre of the picture and observe the lights and shades as part of the process.

This Week's Session

The tasks this week are designed to help you catch a glimpse of the little person who arrived in the world, the circumstances and people who greeted you, and the early stages of your childhood as you went to school and discovered what was going on in the big wide world. The process should mostly be fun. This is not to discount any painful memories you may have. But if you have suffered physical or mental abuse, try to remain objective, and see the underlying pattern in your story. Do not dwell on the emotional side of these issues too much; just focus on why your soul may have chosen these conditions for you. There may be great wisdom behind the choice. For example, the great spiritual coach Dr Wayne D. Dyer spent his childhood in foster homes and orphanages because his father was an alcoholic. But he came to realise that without his difficult childhood he would never have searched for answers to the big issues in life, or have been able to help so many people. Unhappiness is often the gateway to a rich creative or spiritual life. If you need to cry, that's fine, but don't dwell on the painful aspects. You can always confide in your guardian angel, and ask for angelic help with healing the past.

❖ Switch off the phone and create a beautiful environment to work in.
❖ Start your session in your favourite way, by calling on the archangels or creating a power pentagram. Over the next few weeks you will develop your own style for this process: but it is your intention that counts, not the ritual.
❖ Now sit comfortably, relax, close your eyes and visualise yourself going to the sacred building to meet your guardian angel. Ask inwardly:
Dear guardian angel [use his or her name if you have been given one], my aim this week is to remember my childhood hopes and desires and to see that everything that happened was part of my learning process. Support me when I have to face painful old stories and help me to see them in a new light. If there is anything that will help me at this stage, please let me know, either now, or in my dreams.
❖ Now sit quietly for a few moments, giving time for your guardian angel to respond, before beginning your session. Write down any response or insights in your journal.

Tasks for this Session

❖ Collect together the information you have been gathering about your early story and spend a few moments piecing it together in your mind. Did your parents plan to have a baby? Or did they get married in a hurry? Did their parents approve? Were you an only child? Or were you born into an established family where there were already other children? When you were small did you get the impression that you were really loved? Or were you the 'added extra', an afterthought? Were you abandoned and adopted by relatives or strangers?

❖ In your notebook, write a story about yourself in the third person, describing what happened at the time of your birth and during your first five years. This tasks leads off from the brief description you wrote last week but this time you are telling it as a story and writing from another angle, as though the story is about someone else. Put in as much high drama as you can think of. You could start like this, for example:

Janet's mum was not married when Janet was born. Her dad, Jimmy, was in the US army, stationed at Brize Norton in Oxfordshire, and he promised Janet's mum that he would marry her. Marjorie was thrilled to think she would live in America but Jimmy went off, never to return, and left poor Marjorie in England, feeling deserted, an unmarried mother, working as a drudge in her aunt's bed and breakfast, with very little money . . .' and so on.

❖ Read your story out loud to yourself and see if you can add any more drama to the telling of it. Imagine you are writing a soap opera. Then write it out in your journal.

❖ Now think about what happened when you first went to school. Sit for a moment and imagine yourself back in class, then write down any impressions that come up immediately. What subjects did you enjoy? Were there helpful teachers? Were you helped by other people – godparents, neighbours or older children? Did you envy other children who could do things you would have liked to do, or who had possessions you would have liked? Make some notes in your notebook. Highlight the important points, such as discovering a new subject with a really good teacher.

❖ Spend a few minutes remembering your life when you were about seven years old. Who were the 'difficult' people in your life – the people you felt were restrictive, critical or downright unpleasant to you? These attitudes can be very destructive for the growing child but such difficulties are in our lives for a reason, even if we cannot fathom what it is at the time. Critics can turn out to be our best teachers.

❖ Next, try to recall what you liked and what you disliked: include anything you can think of, especially school activities. Children's attitudes are very black and white – 'I like this', 'I don't like that'. This apparent bolshiness helps the child to define him or herself. Parents who try to persuade the child to be an all-rounder, or to enjoy activities that the child dislikes, are overriding natural tendencies. When a child tries to please adults, in order to feel loved and secure, they sometimes deny their own real needs and these become submerged. During this exercise check whether there is any real, heartfelt desire that you have denied. Do you long to do something and when you think about it tears come to your eyes? This emotion is an indicator that you have denied some essence of yourself – perhaps because you felt you could not ask for it without causing ridicule, or some other kind of discomfort.

❖ Now, looking at your present life, identify anything that makes you feel truly passionate. If you could choose only one thing to commit your time to, what would it be?

❖ The final thing to do in this session, before closing down, is to read the section below and make notes of the tasks you need to do in the coming week.

Tasks for the Week

❖ When you make contact with your buddy, read them the story you wrote about your childhood. Try to find several people to read it to. Are you beginning to see your story in a new light?

Perhaps you will find some events less tragic; you may even see some as quite funny. You may get feedback, when the listener points out that perhaps things weren't so tragic after all. Most importantly, do you understand that the story is an essential part of your being, for better or worse?

❖ Find a newspaper for the day you were born. You can easily get hold of the big national papers and you may also be able to see a local paper in your library. What was going on that day? If there was a great celebration like a royal coronation, or a major tragedy such as the declaration of war, this will have affected everyone's mood.

❖ Think about the name you were given. Find out, if you can, why it was chosen. Was it a family name? Were you named after a literary character or a film star? Is it a name that you have to explain – like mine – or is it quite everyday? Did you have a nickname? Has that stuck with you? Do you think you need to grow out of it? Often people shorten a child's name and only use their full name when they are cross. What does your name mean? Do you like its meaning or would you like to change it? During this course you may well decide to reinvent yourself.

Summary

Your childhood story is full of information about your soul's true desires. Have you abandoned them? Can you give yourself permission to follow wholeheartedly the path of your own destiny? Or are you continually distracted by social or other demands? These demands are often put on us when we are still being educated. Schoolteachers and society generally stress that we need certain qualifications in order to make our way in the world. Often adults guide children along a path that seems suitable for the best of reasons but without taking into account the child's temperament. Then, it seems, we are supposed to find lovers and get married and have children and acquire houses and mortgages and bills and . . . and . . . and . . . Do all these 'ands' support your soul? Or do they steal your fire and leave you feeling tired and weary?

For many people the structure of family life creates a sense of safety and of being needed. Being a parent is itself a creative process and many souls choose parenting as part of their journey simply because they can learn so much from having children. But quite often women whose children have grown up discover that they have a real soul calling that they have overlooked, as they were being driven by the biological clock. I have four children and would never suggest that we need to be celibate to follow our soul's path. But as my children developed lives of their own, I discovered that I had talents and desires that were not being acknowledged or explored because family life had taken over; I had neglected my own needs. Now I have the time and opportunity to pursue them.

Men, too, can repress their creative impulses because of the demands of family life. At the ripe age of 42, the painter Paul Gauguin finally left his family and committed himself to the artistic life. I have the impression his family was glad to be rid of him; a passionate artist is not always an easy person to live with. In other cases, choosing not to be a parent is clearly the best path for some souls. One of the messages I shall keep repeating in this course is well put by Shakespeare in his play *Hamlet*: 'There is nothing either good or bad, but thinking makes it so.' Looking at where you are at now, viewing the past and planning the future needs to be done from a position of freedom, without judgement or criticism.

CLOSING DOWN

Before closing down in your favourite way, sit quietly for a moment with your guardian angel. Ask for protection, insight and guidance during this process of uncovering your heart's desire. During the week, share your memories and discoveries: your buddy, or an objective friend, may help you see the funny side of something you have always thought scary or tragic.

Week 3

Reconnecting with Your Soul's Intentions

To be what we are, and to become what we are capable of becoming is the only end of life.
ROBERT LOUIS STEVENSON

This week's aim is to reconnect you with your innermost desires and intentions, so that you will be able to make decisions and plans to support the unfolding of your destiny.

In order to take charge of your life, you have to be clear about your fundamental intentions; you need a fire burning in your heart that will create the light and energy for all your actions. The tasks you have been doing over the last two weeks were designed to help you uncover your childhood inclinations and circumstances. The best possible version of you, and all the possibilities that you can choose to develop, are already there at the moment of your birth, but your family and social environment will certainly have created circumstances that affected your development, at least until you were of an age to make choices for yourself.

Always remember that many people create highly successful lives for themselves under less than perfect conditions. It is entirely up to you whether you accentuate the positive or allow yourself to succumb to negative circumstances. Genes and personal history are givens, but we have the free will to decide how to respond to events. Your strength of purpose will be a key factor in making the most of the cards that your genes and social inheritance have dealt to you.

There are two basic human drives: a Divine or cosmic drive and a social drive. The first comes from our soul, which is driven to evolve and develop its wisdom, so that eventually it can return to its Divine source. The second is driven by the personality or ego, which is an essential tool for survival, so long as we are living in time and in the material world. Before we go to school our Divine nature is dominant because we have not been taught to analyse the world. Children have to be taught to separate and identify, to measure and record, to list and name creatures, plants and objects. And a key concept, introduced early on, is the distinction between 'good' and 'bad'. Children adapt themselves to fit the messages they get from family and school.

Your guardian angel is the messenger of your Divine or cosmic urge and is constantly looking for opportunities to remind you of your soul's needs. When you were young the messages were clearer, because social pressures were less demanding. As your social drive became stronger, you started to pay less attention to inner messages. Maybe, at some point, you will have had a crisis, of health, or money, or in your relationships. Although your guardian angel is loving and generous, sometimes you may walk into a disaster that could have been avoided if only you had listened to inner guidance. Remember that a crisis is an opportunity cleverly designed by heaven to encourage you to rebalance your Divine needs with your social needs. Have you been listening to your angel? And are you heeding the signs?

Sue and Sally's Story

As an astrologer I have often noticed possibilities in natal charts that seem to be unrealised in the adult consulting me. When I gave a chart reading for Sue, a young widow in her late thirties, I noticed a planetary grouping that suggested she might be a performer of some kind. I knew she was a mother with a fairly routine job but I could see that the glamour of singing and dancing might be calling and that maybe she had not acknowledged it. When I asked her about this, Sue's face lit up. She explained that, before she married, from early childhood, she had taken lots of dancing lessons and had been involved in amateur shows. Sue felt that, as a wife and mother, the family should come first and she had given up her theatrical interests when she got married. But now that her husband had died and her children were getting older, I suggested she should allow this latent talent the chance to flower.

On the same day as my session with Sue, I had a second client, a friend of Sue's. Sally had been recently divorced and her children were getting quite independent. I was intrigued to notice that Sally's chart had some similarities to Sue's and I asked her whether she had any interest in singing and dancing. Sally also beamed. 'Oh, yes,' she said, 'I used to go to classes with Sue and we were both in amateur musicals at our local theatre.' She then explained that as well as being good friends they had a family connection and had been more or less like sisters from childhood.

Sue and Sally both thanked me for reminding them of their childhood enthusiasm and promised to get involved in their local amateur dramatic society. In Sue's chart I could also see that she would make a good healer and could do work helping the bereaved. She said she was already training as a counsellor and I explained that her theatrical talents need not compete with this; that singing and dancing would be fun for her and a good counterbalance to working with the bereaved. This story will be one among thousands, of wonderful people who have talents and passions but who feel they cannot realise them because of social expectations.

The Boy and the Falcons

One of my favourite places to visit is a falconry in Oxfordshire, where the staff demonstrate the birds in flight and allow the visitors to participate. I love watching the peregrine falcons, the owls and kestrels as they swoop and dive for the food thrown by the falconer. One day we started talking to the young man who was giving the demonstration – we had seen him there quite a few times in recent visits. He told us with great excitement that he was now working there full time. From a young age he had always had a great passion for the birds of prey and, as a teenager, he would come to the centre as a volunteer helper, getting to know how to feed and weigh the birds. When he left school to start work he got a job as a van driver but he always hoped that he would be able to work with the birds, as his true vocation. He continued to work at the falconry as a volunteer as often as he could fit it in with his working hours.

At last, after several years of making himself really useful, he had been offered a job there and was able to leave his van driving behind. As he spoke, the enthusiasm and joy emanating from this young man was extraordinary – you could almost feel the glow. In the Chinese oracle *I Ching* there is a saying that often recurs: 'Perseverance furthers'. As this course unfolds you will be uncovering any discouraging issues you may have that get in the way of your ability to perservere and achieve your heart's desire.

Whatever your heart's desire, that is what you are in your essence. The heart's desire of an acorn is to be an oak. In one sense the acorn already is the oak; it just hasn't yet unfolded to show itself to the world. This takes time – and we shall be looking at the part time plays in our process at the end of this section. If you have a longing in you, one that hurts when you think about it, this is a sign that there is a part of you that is unsatisfied, something inside you that is bursting to grow and unfold into something wonderful. The best gift you can give the world is to become that wonderful being, a magical, enthusiastic, passionate person – the kind of person other people will want to warm their hands by.

This Week's Session

❖ As usual, switch off the phone and make your room as beautiful as possible. Spend a few minutes using your favourite clearing and protecting techniques.

❖ Now sit comfortably, relax, close your eyes and visualise yourself going to the sacred building to meet your guardian angel. Sit beside your angel and ask inwardly:

Dear guardian angel [use his or her name if you have been given one], help me to uncover the true desires of my soul. My aim this week is to get back in touch with the intentions I had, before I was even born. If there is anything that will help me at this stage, please let me know, either now, or in my dreams.

❖ Sit quietly for a few moments, giving time for your guardian angel to respond. Describe anything important in your journal.

Tasks for this Session

❖ Draw a big red heart on a large sheet of paper. On another piece of paper make a list of at least 20 words that come immediately to mind when someone asks you 'What are you heart's desires?' These words could be quite abstract. Marilyn Monroe said, 'I just want to be wonderful.' Each new human being brings something special into the world: what do you want to bring – beauty, fun, healing, happiness? But specifics are important; Marilyn wanted to be wonderful by being a glamorous movie star, not by being Mother Teresa. Look at all the words you have written and choose one to write in the centre of your heart. Then create six mini-hearts around the edge of the big one and write in these six more words from your list.

❖ Take some time to think about what is going on in your life and consider whether you are near or far from achieving your heart's desires. You could imagine that you are like Dorothy, in *The Wizard of Oz*, on her journey to the Emerald City – have you gone to sleep in the poppy field? Or can you see your goal on the horizon? Are you on the right path? Are you in touch with your guardian angel (perhaps Toto was Dorothy's angel) and have you got human helpers and supporters?

❖ Try this visualisation: Imagine you are back in your sacred building, the one you found when you went on the journey to meet your guardian angel. Ask your guardian angel to take you back in time so that you can remember what you hoped for and longed for, before you were born. Your guardian wraps you in soft wings and lifts you to a beautiful, peaceful place, beyond the world. You can see the earth below and you know you are waiting to be born into a new human life. Spend some time meditating and visualising the way you truly want to be in the world and how you want the world to experience the you that you really are. Now, imagine there is nothing to stop you unfolding your true destiny. Can you see what it would be? Ask your guardian angel to bring you back to your sacred space and then gently ground yourself.

Tasks for the Week

❖ Think about the things you liked when you were young – the books you enjoyed, the films that enthralled you and the music you listened to. Did the wild call to you, through books about jungles and rain forests? Were you fascinated by courtroom dramas, fantasising about delivering great defence speeches? Or did you hang your teenage room with black and purple, because you were into magic and mystery? What did you collect? Were you sporty or bookish? Although adults often say that children are going 'through phases', these obsessions give you clues to some deep desire – if it was 'just a phase', that might be because you didn't have the opportunity to follow it through.

❖ Start an I LOVE scrapbook, and collect pictures of anything that appeals to you – of far-off places, animals, works of art, a designer bedroom, lovely clothes. Choose images that definitely give you the tingle factor. You will gradually notice a particular theme developing and this theme will provide more clues to any hidden desires.

❖ Find a photograph of yourself as a young child, as early as possible. Chinese doctors say that the essence of what we are shines out when we are babies and that we should always have early pictures of ourselves around, to remind ourselves of our inner divinity. Make a collage using the photograph in the centre. Surround your picture with other images that seem important – some might come from your I LOVE collection. You could create thought bubbles, like the ones you see in cartoons, and draw sketches representing things that your little self was dreaming about.

❖ Identify five events during your childhood, from birth to ten years old – or while you were still at junior school – that made an impression on you at the time. Ask yourself whether any of those events are connected with your heart's desires. For example, when I was about ten, a benefactor presented our school with a big basket of theatrical costumes. I had never seen anything so wonderful, except on the cinema news, when the Queen was crowned in glorious Technicolor. This prompted me to write a school play which was performed by the other pupils. Later on in life, I designed wedding dresses and ball gowns, and worked on theatrical costumes.

❖ Make some time during the week to go through the Review of Part 1 below. This is designed to make sure you have not missed anything important in the process so far.

REVIEW OF PART 1 – FIRE

Look back at the exercises you completed in Weeks 1, 2 and 3, then answer the following questions:

1 Do you feel you can now look at your family history as a necessary background for your present life?
2 Do you understand that the difficulties you may have had with people as a child, whether family, friends, or teachers, were part of your chosen story, reflecting back to you your soul's need to grow and learn?
3 Do you feel you are now in touch with your heart's desire and with your guardian angel?

If the answer to questions 1 and 2 is no, then allow some time during the coming week to go back to some of the exercises in Weeks 1 and 2 and repeat the ones that call to you. If the answer to 3 is no, then also allow time to repeat the visualisation on page 65.

Summary

When we look at the passions of our childhood we may catch glimpses of the hopes and desires that we arrived with. Just as a bud on a rose tree holds the petals that will unfold and bloom as a rose, the child also carries the beauty of its inner potential. Because this potential has a drive to unfold, there is a magical energy field at work, calling events and people towards the growing child. This magical energy field is your guardian angel, who attracts what you need towards you, especially when you are small. The basket of theatre costumes did not *cause* me to want to get involved in costume and plays; it awoke a latent talent that was simply waiting (in the wings, we might say) for the right possibility to arrive. If I had been a natural botanist I would probably have been drawn to the school garden.

Although modern psychology encourages us to think that childhood events cause us to develop in a particular way, people who raise children often notice that the opposite seems true – that something mysterious in the nature of the child seems to call certain events towards it. As a mother of four, I can say that even before birth a mother picks up messages at an unconscious level about the soul who is coming into life through her. The incoming soul calls out to the parents to choose the right name for it. It is the soul that chooses the time and place of birth – so if you, or anyone else you know, was born at an unexpected time or place, you can be sure there was a good reason for it. You can also be sure that the children who are described as 'difficult' behave badly because something they need is missing – they may not even understand what it is, or be able to ask for it.

Let me tell you a little story. There is a man living in a gatehouse that belongs to a princess who lives in the mansion at the end of a long drive. The gatekeeper is so busy opening and closing the gates, watching out for visitors, looking after the house and garden, and so on, that he has forgotten that the house he lives in belongs to the princess, who is the real source of abundance in his life. The princess keeps sending her messenger boy along the drive to remind the servant to keep in touch, so that she can give him exactly what he needs without him having to struggle. But the servant is so busy rushing around that he doesn't listen to the messages.

The man in this story is your ego, the princess is your soul, and the princess's messenger is your guardian angel. If only you would stop to listen to the messages from your guardian angel, you would receive all the blessings you need to live a happy and fulfilled life. The most wonderful things can happen when your ego and your guardian angel are working as a team. This course is designed to help you reinstate that relationship.

As you work through the suggested tasks, you will gradually find it easier to see what in your life is a perfect fit and what needs changing.

You have now completed the first three weeks of the course and I hope you now feel more in touch with your own inner fire and with your guardian angel. Don't worry if you feel that you have not got the whole picture yet; there are plenty more opportunities during the rest of the course for your soul's code to become clear.

CLOSING DOWN

Remember to ground yourself before returning to your ordinary activities. Whatever grounding ritual you have chosen for yourself, do not get into a habit of rushing it. Gently adjusting yourself to the outer world pays dividends, because it allows your new insights to stabilise deep in your psyche. Say thank you to your guardian angel before putting out the candle. You can include sending blessings to your loved ones at the end of each session as well.

Interlude

Old Father Time

But at my back I always hear
Time's wingèd chariot hurrying near
ANDREW MARVELL

I want you to spend some time thinking about Time. I once heard someone say, 'We have to have time, so that everything doesn't happen at once.' Time is a vital ingredient in the creative process, whether you are writing a book, painting a picture, growing a garden or creating a life that you love. And in today's world we all tend to feel short of time; commercial and economic pressures often reduce the time we have to ourselves – time to do our inner work, as well as time to do our outer work, with care and full attention.

Even if we have a sense that part of us is timeless, we have to work in the world of time. How much time we have available to carry out our life purpose we cannot know. We may take precautions to stay alive as long as possible – treat our bodies with care, look both ways when we cross the road – but something unpredictable can arrive out of the blue to end everything. Which is why the Sufis tell us to live each moment as though we had a thousand years but also be prepared to leave at any moment.

The mythical figure of Old Father Time is a rather dour old man carrying an hourglass and a scythe, reminding us of both the constant passage of time and that life can be swiftly cut off (he is similar to the the Grim Reaper). He comes down to us from Greek mythology, where he is known as Kronos, or Chronos (the name gives us the word 'chronological'). He was originally the chief of the gods and the Romans called him Saturn.

Kronos' parents were the sky god Ouranos (the Roman Uranus) and the earth goddess Gaia. The myth tells us that Gaia gave birth to many children; Ouranos kept her constantly pregnant, so that she never had time to nurture her babies. The last three were monsters whom the horrified Ouranos hid deep in the ground. Furious, Gaia gave her youngest son Kronos a sickle which he used to emasculate his father (separating the sky from the earth). This rather unpleasant story does have one beautiful outcome: from this act of violence, foam fell into the sea from which the goddess Aphrodite, the Roman Venus, was born, rising from the ocean in a seashell.

Kronos became a serious tyrant and an oracle prophesied that one of his own children would overthrow him. To prevent this, Kronos swallowed all his children at birth. Eventually, his long-suffering wife, Rhea, tricked him; when the baby Zeus was born she wrapped a stone in swaddling clothes and Kronos swallowed it, thinking he had put paid to another potential threat. The baby Zeus was hidden in a cave in Crete and grew up to supplant his father as the greatest god on Mount Olympus. In Roman mythology Zeus became Jupiter, with the title Optimus Maximus, meaning 'the greatest and best'. After that, Kronos took second place.

The reason myths like this are helpful to us on our journey is that they explain the human relationship with time. Constantly giving birth, Gaia never had time to love and nurture her children. The name Zeus means 'enlightener' or 'he who brings enlightenment'. When we become enlightened we see that time is an illusion and that our minds are contributing to the illusion since we create our 'reality' with our thoughts. If time takes over to the extent that we are always clock watching, then we are allowing time to become a tyrant and nothing gets created. We need to realise that time is not our master, but our servant.

Time present and time past
Are both perhaps present in time future,
T.S. ELIOT

When we take mastery over our own lives time becomes less of
an issue and we can expect to have exactly enough time to do what
we need to do. We often hear of creative artists who are finishing
a great masterpiece living long enough to complete their work: living
becomes an act of will. If you intend to live a long and happy life,
and feel certain of your inner power to choose, I believe you will
achieve your intention. The inner power of your conviction creates
an energy field that resists all kinds of outside forces. Who chooses
whether you live or die under certain circumstances? Who decides
how much time you have, in order to fulfil your life purpose? You
do. I cannot prove this to you beyond any doubt but I suggest you
behave as though this is true and see how this idea changes your
attitude to life. This change in attitude will, in turn, change how
your life unfolds.

What is this life if, full of care,
We have no time to stand and stare.
W.H. DAVIES

Think about how time changes for you, as you grow from a tiny
baby to a working adult. When we are small we are innocent of
time and can play with no sense of limitation. Then, gradually, we
are socialised by family and school. By about seven years old, we
have been trained to understand time and the concepts of past and
future. We leave behind the mystical state of innocence when we
experienced the world directly, without mentally chopping our existence up into time frames. Many processes in school life affect our
relationship with time. Often children are hurried along and not
allowed to take their time over tasks. Intelligence is measured by
tests that have to be answered at speed. Even exams in creative
subjects are often limited by time – how much can you write about
the greater spotted woodpecker in three minutes? Might it not be

more fulfilling to spend the whole day thinking about the wood-pecker and then writing a wonderful poem about it? Everyone has a right to take their time – it belongs to them, and to no one else.

In the second seven years of life, we grow into teenagers and time becomes even more of an issue. School rules and timetables seem designed to bind us into uncreative situations, in which the mind is being disciplined to suit society, rather than the individual child. No wonder teenagers protest. Part of them is shouting, 'Help, get me out of here! I am losing touch with my soul!' Parents and teachers only want the best for children but what is best for one is not best for another. Adults may not realise that the most disrup-tive children are often the most creative ones.

The hands of the clock keep turning . . . Another seven years and we may get married and have children or we may dedicate ourselves to a demanding career. Invariably in Western society, we get drawn into 'must have' materialism and start taking out loans for our first car, or our first flat. When we take out a loan we are selling our future time; the word 'mortgage' actually means 'engaged unto death'.

By the time we reach 30 we are settled into adult life and our youth can seem a long way away. We may have a crisis of self. What is going on? How are we using our time in this incarnation? An illness, such as depression or ME, which disconnects you from the hustle and bustle of everyday life, can be an indicator that your soul is calling you to take the time to reconnect with your life purpose. If we survive our thirties unscathed, we may have to face our real issues when we get into our forties in a classic mid-life crisis. The fact that these turning points are accompanied by depres-sion and self-doubt indicates that we are living unsatisfactory lives.

Work, work, work all day;
work work, work all night,
work 'til you can't tell wrong from right.
WILL SHAMAN

Why are we are always trying to fit more and more things into shorter and shorter periods of time? In a materialistic society, economic, and therefore physical, survival seems to depend on working under ever greater levels of stress. Past generations were told that the development of technology would create more leisure time but nowadays the existence of the computer means that people never switch off. The concept of setting aside at least one day a week as a day of rest, when we can take stock of our lives, has almost completely disappeared.

Many people still look forward to enjoying their retirement but what a pity not to recognise that you have choices *now* about how you use your days. In order to live life to the full and realise your true vision of yourself, you need to develop a sense of certainty about who you are and what you are doing. With that certainty comes a release of tension, because if you have an accurate assessment of what has to be done, there will always be enough time in which to do it. Time does not run out. Despite appearances, we have exactly enough time to do what we need to do.

Working with your guardian angel reminds you of your connection to the timeless world. Regularly taking that inner journey allows you to step outside the busyness of your everyday world and sit quietly in a place of peace and delight, where you can stop doing and just be. And this time is never 'wasted'. It has a profound effect on the rest of your life: things fall into place more easily, problems dissolve and you feel more secure and confident. Take your time – it is your own – and use it wisely.

PART 2

The World of
Information – Air

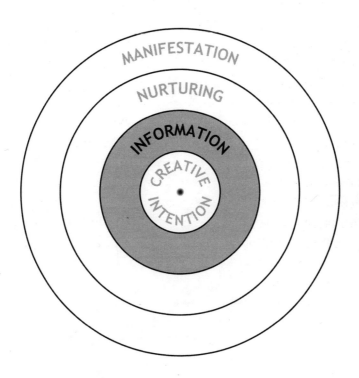

The World of Information – Air

This most excellent canopy, the air . . .
WILLIAM SHAKESPEARE

Now that you have identified your passions, the next step is to give thought to how to bring them into reality. So we move from the realm of Fire into the realm of Air – the world of thought and information. In classical and medieval times, philosophers described the angels as 'intelligences', meaning that they belonged to the realm of ideas.

According to Plato, everything that exists has an idea that supports it and there is a perfect idea underlying everything, even if the actual reality is not perfect. Your soul's code is the perfect idea of who you can be, even if you are not able to live up to this ideal. Our lives can never be absolutely perfect because we do not live in the airy realm but we can work towards bringing the ideal into everyday reality. Becoming aware of your thoughts and how they affect your life choices, both great and small, is essential to fulfilling your soul's code.

Thought allows us to process information, and information is exactly what is needed during the second stage of the creative process. One meaning of the verb 'to inform' is to put form into something. Any vision needs some information in order for the imaginary to become reality. Think of a dress designer who has an inspiration for a wonderful ball gown: she needs to give the information as a fashion sketch, to the pattern cutter. Similarly, an architect with a vision for a new skyscraper, has to draw up plans to inform the builders. So, too, your heart's desire needs first to be clearly stated; then it has to be considered and developed into a clearly defined plan. Only then will you know what you are aiming for and, ultimately, whether you have succeeded.

DNA is an example of information that provides instructions for a growing baby to acquire particular characteristics – red hair, long legs and so on. When you were born, your soul carried an image of what it wanted to be but this information was clouded by contact with the outside world – it is a most unusual person who is able to maintain that sense of soul purpose in the face of social pressures. The story of Jesus, who was found talking knowledgeably with the temple priests when he was only 12, suggests that he remembered his own destiny very clearly indeed. When our sense of purpose is clear, then we know exactly what choices to make, and these choices empower us to create a life that we love.

AIR – The ancients chose the element of air to symbolise thought, which is intangible but, like air, has an effect on the world around it. Air is invisible, yet it contains mysterious currents – breezes that can carry leaves, feathers and paper, or winds and gales that can move branches from trees and roofs from houses.

Air also symbolises communication – we speak of airing our opinions and the radio is 'on the air'. Sound travels through air and we make sounds in order to communicate: these sounds can be just noises of pain or delight or they can be structured sentences. But we also have an ability to communicate silently, sending messages mind to mind. We are not very good at this and our technological tools like telephones and the Internet discourage us from bothering to practise telepathy.

According to ancient thought, the gods and the angels lived in the airy realms; they could move without effort, flying with winged heels between heaven and earth. The primary task of an angel is to bring messages – *angelos* is the Greek word for messenger. And messages can be delivered speedily between the Divine and the

---

earthly realms because air offers no resistance. Air is cool, pure and definitely unearthly.

The ancients believed air, like fire, had Divine qualities. The highest qualities in a human were spirit (fire) and mind (air). At death we would leave behind our physical shell, created from water and earth, and ascend to heaven through the upper air. In Shakespeare's play, Cleopatra expresses this in her dying speech: 'I am fire and air; my other elements [water and earth] I give to baser life.'

Throughout history, humans have sought to conquer the air. Leonardo da Vinci was designing flying machines in the fifteenth century, although it has taken us a little longer to achieve his vision. Now we have created aeroplanes that speed up travel, and rockets that can penetrate even the upper atmosphere, we are able to explore the places where the ancient gods were believed to reside. As a result, we have polluted the atmosphere, the very breath of our life, and we will have to work hard to clear it, just as we need to work hard to clear our cluttered thoughts in order truly to know our own purpose in life.

Your thoughts can be reactions to circumstances, for example: 'I am happy that my favourite film star won an Oscar,' or 'I am tired of listening to that dreadful music played by my neighbours.' But the most important function of thought is creative: in order to develop a life worthy of your soul you need to clear out the petty thoughts that are just reactions to what you like or dislike and replace them with creative thoughts that serve a definite purpose. I once heard of a scientist who refused to read other people's books or academic papers, because he did not want his own mind cluttered with their thought processes. He felt he could think more clearly, and be more original, if he allowed his own mind free rein. And it is often the case that original thinkers – writers, poets, artists, inventors – have followed their own path, ignoring the influences of other people. During this next part of the course you will be checking out how far your life has been influenced by other people.

Our relationship with the world, and all the other people we encounter, is entirely governed by the way we think about ourselves and about reality. If events in our childhood suggested that the world was a dangerous place, then we may have continued to think like that, even after the events were long over. It is true that the world presents dangers, but those dangers have mostly been created out of human fears and anxieties. Great spiritual traditions tell us that even natural disasters are caused by the state of human consciousness. Because we are all part of Gaia, the spirit of the earth, the way earthlings think, as well as the way they behave, has an effect on the planet on which we live.

I hope that by now you have begun to feel some kind of stirring deep in your heart, perhaps the feeling that something that was lying dormant in your soul is beginning to wake up. The answers to the questions, 'Who am I? And what am I supposed to be doing here?' may not be blindingly obvious yet but this course provides a process that offers your soul the opportunity to reconnect with your guardian angel, so that your path becomes gradually clearer.

During this second stage of the course you will be retrieving important information which will involve doing some more research. In Week 4 you will be identifying choices that you made earlier in life and investigating how you have been thinking about yourself. These thoughts and choices have brought you to your present position. By unpicking the stories and events of your early life and young adulthood, you will begin to see which choices have been useful and which ones may have led you down a blind alley.

The Divine power, God, the source of life, whatever term you prefer, begins the act of creation with an intense will to manifest itself. This is the world of fire, where the seraphim fan the Divine fire with their many wings and maintain a constant vibration to support it, by singing *kadosh, kadosh, kadosh* – holy, holy, holy. In the second world, the world of air, it is the turn of the archangels to work with the creator's vision, putting in place the basic structures that will allow the vision to unfold. Each archangel has a different quality that adds to the whole.

In Week 5, you will be looking at the seven basic purposes that human beings arrive with, deciding which one best fits your own soul's story. This will lead you to Week 6, which is all about asking whether your present life allows you to express your underlying purpose. This will enable you to formulate new strategies and plans, designed to create the best opportunity for your soul to achieve its highest potential.

Week 4

Choices You Have Made

All you have to do is decide what to do with the time you are given.
J.R.R. TOLKIEN, The Lord of the Rings

This week's aim is to take stock of your past choices and present thoughts about your life. Whatever is going on for you at present is the result of choices you have made, consciously or unconsciously. Do your past choices support your life purpose? The explorations you will make over the next three weeks are designed to help you form conscious choices that will determine how things will unfold from here on.

Many of your early life choices were made during your school years, which may not have been the best years of your life. Shakespeare describes the boy 'creeping unwillingly to school', and Wordsworth speaks of a prison-house closing in on the growing child. If we look at the history of education we can see that the adults in charge may have started with the best of intentions for the needs of growing children but that some of their methods have been misguided. I am not suggesting that all education is negative but early training does create the bedrock on which you have built your understanding of the world and, in the case of Western education, this training is based on a view of reality that does not always encourage freedom for your individual soul's needs.

Originally, schooling was just for the rich, who trained their children (chiefly boys) in physical sports, languages and the classics, so that the new generation could perpetuate the traditions of their own aristocratic class. In Victorian Britain, public education was created by the Church, hand in glove with the State; both institutions had their own reasons for providing free schools. The reasons were economic and social; schools were in a position to train young minds to accept the status quo and, at the same time, to make sure that the next generation of workers had the right skills for the needs of the capitalist society. Do I sound like a revolutionary? Well, I have to admit that I am one . . . but not in the usual political sense. This book is intended to revolutionise the way you think about yourself and to encourage you to rethink your options.

As a schoolchild, one of your basic choices was between being keen on schoolwork or being a reluctant student. As early as five years old a child can make a decision about its future without realising it; a close friend of mine told me that as soon as he went through the gate on his first day of primary school he knew he was in a place that was not good for him. Although he was inquisitive about the world, curious and bright, the classroom felt like a place of restriction which limited his desire to explore the world at his own pace. The comedian Billy Connolly makes hilarious jokes about being taught algebra, for which he could see absolutely no purpose – it may be useful for a future theoretical physicist but not for a future comedy king. And this is where the problem lies: how can schoolteachers know who they are teaching? They are not aware of your soul's code. And, as a young child, nor were you. But you will have had instincts about your likes and dislikes and, depending on your character, you will have made these clear to the adults around you.

The young Pablo Picasso infuriated his schoolteachers because he absolutely refused to do anything except painting and drawing. We often hear educators talk about 'an all-round education' but the genius in each one of us would love the chance to be totally absorbed – obsessed even – by our own true vocation. That vocation may not be something as grand as becoming a world-class artist like Picasso but, whatever it is, it is important that you do it – no, not important: ESSENTIAL.

As you became a teenager you were asked to make decisions about what subjects you would take at exam level and possibly take on to higher education. Sometimes the subjects offered may not have included a possibility for you – there was no astrology on my school curriculum. You may have been tempted by the idea that training in secretarial work or information technology would be a passport to a regular income. If you are a woman, you may have been much more focused on eventually having children than on something you really wanted for yourself – Mother Nature uses all kinds of tricks to make sure the human race keeps reproducing. This week you will be thinking about your early choices, and what or who influenced those choices.

A Talent Found, Lost and Found Again

When Patrick was five he used to watch *Top of the Pops* and jump up and down using a hockey stick as a pretend guitar. When he was 14, his mum bought him a real guitar and he taught himself to play in his bedroom without an instruction manual, simply learning from an old record by a folk singer. Patrick's dad didn't approve of *Top of the Pops* or electric guitars but folk guitar was definitely Good, with a capital G. So Dad encouraged Patrick to develop his guitar playing and in the process discovered a latent talent of his own – writing the words for folk songs. They started to play together in their folk clubs and Patrick experienced the thrill of captivating an audience with his playing.

So far, so good. We can see that the guardian angel has been prompting all the characters in this story. The mother is following her intuition and has given Patrick exactly what he needs. The father is taking a lead from this and developing his own gift as well as helping Patrick move forward. Patrick himself can't get enough of music and, like any budding genius, would prefer to spend all his time playing his guitar rather than doing homework. But social forces are about to put a dampener on what could have quickly developed as a brilliant career.

At school Patrick's musical talent went unnoticed – only classical music was acceptable at the grammar school. But Patrick was also a reasonably talented artist and this was suggested as a career – not to become an artist, of course, but an art teacher. So often, sensible adults suggest a child could teach something instead of doing it. No one ever suggested that the music could ever be more than a hobby. It was not until Patrick was over 30 that he realised that he could not only play guitar to a high standard, for which he might actually get paid, but that he too could write great song lyrics. By that time he had been trained as a book designer and had a wife and family to support, so changing direction was almost impossible. Now in his mid forties, Patrick still works part time as a designer but writes songs for his part-time band and for musical theatre. The tide is beginning to turn in favour of the music: one of his shows has had a professional production so, if he keeps focused on his desire, he may well be able to give up the design work before too long.

One of the curious aspects of this story is that Patrick's dad seemed to play a positive role; but when we look more closely we can see that he wanted Patrick to play only a certain kind of music. Dad's interest was a double-edged sword. Another boy might have found some local mates to play music with, giving him more freedom to experiment and to find a wider audience. In addition, Patrick was so in awe of his father's gift for writing the words that, for many years, he thought his own talent was just for composing. It was not until he was nearly 30 that he discovered he could write his own lyrics. However, he tells me that he learned a great deal about the structure of verses and creating interesting rhyming patterns from his dad.

Alex Makes His Own Choice

Alex was obviously gifted from childhood. He learned to speak early and, when he went to school, he always got top marks in all subjects. He was equally capable in the arts and the sciences. And he was an excellent musician. He learned to play the clarinet and the piano and always got distinctions in music exams. Alex's mother was especially thrilled with his musical talent because she herself had longed to play an instrument as a child and her family had been too poor to enable this.

Alex's music teacher was greatly impressed by the prodigy in his care and had a meeting with Alex's parents, suggesting that their son was not only good enough to join the National Youth Orchestra, but was a good candidate for a scholarship at a specialist school for gifted musicians. In a situation like this, Alex could have been pressurised by parents and teacher into following a musical career. But he didn't want to follow this path and his parents were wise enough not to try to influence his decision. Eventually he became a scientist, with his own laboratory in a university. Sometimes he appears on television, talking about his specialist subject. Alex still plays music, for his own pleasure, and supports his children who are both learning to play instruments.

Youngsters do not have to be as unusually gifted as Alex to be placed in a similar quandary. Often parents are so keen for their children to live out their own lost dreams that a child can be swamped by parental enthusiasm and be unable to listen to their own dream. If you are bringing up children yourself, look for the signs of their natural abilities, encourage them and support their interests but don't force them into becoming something you wanted for yourself. If you have a lost dream, there is always time to recover it, in some measure, in your own way.

This Week's Session

❖ Prepare your room in the usual way. Don't forget to switch off that phone! This is your time, for your sacred inner work.

❖ Now sit comfortably, relax, close your eyes and visualise yourself once more sitting beside your guardian angel in your sacred building. Ask for your angel's help:
Dear guardian angel [use his or her name if you have been given one], support me while I examine the choices I have made, especially choices I made early in my life. Allow me to recall my reasons for making the choices, and let me see clearly those occasions when I failed to follow my intuition and listened to the voices of others. If there is anything

that will help me at this stage, please let me know, either now, or in my dreams.

❖ Sit quietly for a few moments, giving time for your guardian angel to respond. Remember to record anything significant in your journal.

Tasks for this Session

❖ In your journal, list some of the career suggestions that other people gave you when you were younger: in one column list ideas that were helpful, in a second column list those that you feel hindered you. For example: in the positive column you might include: 'If you work hard to develop your artistic ability [or whatever gift you had], then you will be able to earn a good living.' On the negative side you might have: 'Music is only suitable as a hobby, you won't be able to earn a living doing that – better get a teaching qualification instead.'

❖ Looking at the second column, ask yourself whether you still believe those negative ideas, and if you do, create your own affirmations to contradict them. One excellent affirmation, which you can use to squash all negative thoughts and bolster self-esteem, is: THE UNIVERSE SUPPORTS ME IN CREATING A LIFE THAT I CHOOSE FOR MYSELF.

❖ Spend some time recalling the ideas you had when you were young about what you wanted for yourself in life. Do you remember seeing someone else doing something that you strongly wanted to do yourself and felt that you could do it, and do it really well?

❖ Recall any activities, school subjects, books, television programmes or movies that attracted you. Think about the objects you had in your bedroom when you were old enough to choose your own possessions. Now imagine that you are ten years old. You have been given a small chest in which to create a time capsule to show someone in the future what was once important to you. Into your chest put anything that represents your ten-year-old self: include anything to do with your favourite activities, hobbies, school subjects and maybe a favourite book or video.

❖ Now imagine opening this box as your present-day self. When you look at the contents do you think, 'That was just a passing phase', or do you find yourself wishing you had developed one of your interests further? Do you notice anything that was an early indication of a gift that would develop later? At that age I was keen on sewing; I used to buy dolls from the local Woolworths and dress them up. My favourite styles included a nurse, a bride and a Queen Elizabeth I costume. As an adult, I worked for several years as a dress designer, creating bridal gowns and theatrical costumes, though no nurses' uniforms. Although I no longer do this kind of work for a living, I always get a real thrill when I am in a fabric store and I still make my own clothes.

❖ Now mentally repack your box. Leave out anything that is no longer important, update anything that has developed to a more grown-up stage and add anything new that has appeared since you were ten.

❖ Identify any choices you made between the age of ten and the present that led to your neglecting an activity that was once important to you. Say, for example, that one of the items in your box is a tennis racquet; you enjoyed tennis at school and getting picked for the team. You used to watch Wimbledon and imagined yourself on the Centre Court, winning the match. But now you don't play at all. Why did you stop? Did someone say: 'Not everyone can get to the top?' That is a classic disempowering remark that adults make to young people. My granddaughters have always enjoyed performing and it would be easy to cloud their vision by pointing out that not everyone can be Britney Spears. What I say to them is that plenty of people make good money in the music business even if they are not as famous as Britney. I also tell them that if they keep a fire alight in their own hearts, follow their intuition and work hard, then their desire will become a magnet for good opportunities. Luck, I tell them, is what happens when you believe in yourself and follow your path with courage.

Tasks for the Week

❖ During the week, collect cuttings from magazines of any pictures that represent your present-day dreams, your vision of the way you would like to be. Save these in your folder for next week's session.

❖ Refer to the list of choices you made in your journal and see if you can make contact with anyone who was in your life at the time you were making them. Can you talk to someone in the family? Or a former teacher? This will give you an opportunity to discuss and perhaps get a new perspective on what was going on at that time. You may well see that it was the only choice you could make, under those circumstances.

❖ Every time you notice a negative thought such as, 'I should have done this instead of that', or 'I should have listened to my intuition', remind yourself that you made choices based on limited understanding. Write affirmations that reassure you that from now on your choices will be made with a clearer vision, for example: NOW I KNOW HOW TO WORK WITH MY GUARDIAN ANGEL AND MAKE CHOICES THAT SUPPORT MY HIGHEST POSSIBILITY.

❖ Make notices to pin up in your house, or place by your desk, using this affirmation and the one I gave you earlier: THE UNIVERSE SUPPORTS ME IN CREATING A LIFE THAT I CHOOSE FOR MYSELF.

Summary

You may know the song, '*Que sera, sera*, Whatever will be will be. The future's not ours to see.' It is true that we cannot see the future precisely, because the future is not fixed. We are constantly creating the future as we go along. In Charles Dickens's story *A Christmas Carol*, the miserly Ebenezer Scrooge is visited by three spirits – the Spirit of Christmas Past, the Spirit of Christmas Present and the Spirit of Christmas Future. The third spirit shows Scrooge a dreadful future, based on his present behaviour but the spirit also shows him that if he can change his ways the future will be different. Bad-tempered, stingy old Ebenezer is so shocked by the vision of his potential future that he turns over a new leaf and becomes generous and loving towards his fellow humans.

Right now, today, you are creating your future. Your actions create your destiny. Your actions are based on your reactions and responses to circumstances, events and people, and also on your ideas – about who you are and how much or how little power you have to realise the best in yourself. The fact that you are reading this book may indicate that you are still uncertain about yourself and your place in the world. These uncertainties may be around because you were taught that you had to fit into the world around you, choosing only from the limited number of possibilities that school and society presented you with.

When I arrived at school-leaving age my elders and betters suggested I should go into the Civil Service, a long-term career with a good pension. I made the mistake of listening to the voices of reason. Brown corridors, dirty green filing cabinets and piles of beige paper: I was starved of beauty, intellectually bored and emotionally frustrated by work that did not engage my soul at any level. I was like a captain sailing a ship without a map. I had no awareness then that there might be an inner navigator – my guardian angel, who would be able to help me understand my true vision. With this help I would be able to map out a wise path, and keep faith with my vision. My guardian would also nudge me whenever outside influences distracted me from it. It took me many years to discover that this help was a reality.

At the beginning of the twenty-first century we are much more aware of having a variety of choices and the media has popularised the idea of 'reinventing' oneself. This idea is really useful; we invented our relationship with the world in the first place, so we can certainly change our hairstyles, the way we dress, how we spend our time and who we mix with. We cannot change who we are at a fundamental level – a banana tree will never grow apples. But if the banana tree has not produced any fruit for years, because it has the mistaken idea that it should be growing apples, then it is time to ask the universe for some banana-friendly compost. If you feel you were a seed that fell on stony ground, so that your needs and desires never received the nutrients that would encourage growth and fruitfulness, now is the time to tend your garden and give your seedlings some tender loving care.

CLOSING DOWN

Before closing down in your favourite way, sit quietly with your guardian angel. Ask for protection, insight and reassurance. Ask to be reminded that old choices are not mistakes but part of your learning process. During the week, share your stories with a friend or a family member. Often you will find that people will be happy to tell you their own experiences of choices they made along the way and you may be able to help them to gain new insights.

Week 5

The Information You Need

If the angel comes to you, it will be because you have
convinced her, not by your tears, but by your humble resolve
to be always beginning: to be a beginner.
RAINER MARIA RILKE

This week's aim is to identify your underlying purpose in life. When you build a house, the foundation stone must be in place before you can start raising the walls. In the same way, your fundamental purpose is a foundation stone for a satisfying life. If you think carefully about the life of any successful person, whether someone you know or someone famous, you will find that they are fuelled by a sense of purpose that provides the foundation for their life. And if you are not already aware of yours, this is the week when you will find it.

In searching for the essential ingredients in your soul's code, you need to identify the starting point. Where do you begin? Every human being offers a unique contribution to the development of human consciousness and the unique code that is yours will have at its core one simple need. As well as the drive for physical survival, the human soul has other primary needs: the need to create beauty, the need to relate to others, the need to communicate and so on. We all have these needs in different proportions and your sense of purpose and commitment grow from a sense of certainty of your own primary need.

I believe we can identify seven basic purposes, from which a multitude of beautiful variations emerge, as each individual human takes up the true purpose of his or her own life story. Think of the musical scale, which has seven notes – how many wonderful pieces of music can be created just from seven notes! Each of us is creating a unique song, contributing to the magnificent concert of the human story. Here are the seven basic purposes:

To create, to bring new inspiration into the world: includes the creative arts and also everyday creativity, such as creating a beautiful home.

To protect, to nurture and encourage: includes stewardship of our planet, as well as caring for children, animals or creative projects.

To heal, to soothe and reconcile: includes healing and reconciliation at a personal level, for oneself, or one's immediate family.

To transform, to act as a catalyst for change: the change can be personal or social.

To teach, to communicate or transmit: includes higher wisdom and spiritual truth, and also practical skills and social values.

To lead, to inspire and invigorate: bringing enthusiasm and vision to individuals and groups.

To organise, to manage and create structures: provides the foundation on which to build individual and social projects.

Associated with these seven purposes are seven of the greatest archangels. One of this week's tasks is a visualisation that will help you identify your own basic purpose. When you understand your purpose you can work with the appropriate archangel, as well as with your guardian angel.

PURPOSE	ARCHANGEL
To create	Gabriel
To protect	Auriel (she has a companion called Sandalphon)
To heal	Raphael
To transform	Hanael
To teach	Zadkiel
To lead	Michael
To organise	Samael

You will have noticed that I refer to Auriel (sometimes spelled Uriel) as she. The angels and archangels do not have any gender – how could they, as they have no physical bodies? It is traditional, though to my mind old fashioned, to refer to them all as 'he'. Unfortunately, we do not have a suitable pronoun to replace 'he or she' and 'it' seems impersonal. So my habit is to use either 'he' or 'she', depending on the primary role of the archangel. For example, Raphael carries a healing and reconciling energy that we humans experience as 'feminine' although, of course, the role of healer has often been undertaken by men. Revolution and change are associated with masculine energy, so Hanael, who is a warrior angel, can be called 'he'. I suggest you choose whether to use 'he' or 'she' according to your personal experiences with the archangels. Just do not fall into the trap of thinking that all Divine or angelic beings are male. In these modern times we should be experiencing the angels directly and evaluating our own experience, not relying on medieval concepts based on feudal social structures.

Recently one of my students sent in an assignment for the home study foundation course I offer. Jane had not been following the course you are doing now and had not seen this list of basic purposes, but from her own inner work she had realised this underlying law for herself. She wrote:

> *These Archangels represent vocational types that one can meet in everyday life. We all know people who fit into these categories: Raphael the born healer, Gabriel the artist or poet, and Michael the born leader, etc.*

I want to draw your attention to an important spiritual law: that all these purposes are interdependent. We may identify our purpose as 'to lead' but as a leader we need someone to work with us who can organise, otherwise our project will go off like a damp squib. And the organiser needs someone to create the projects for him or her to organise. If you look at the list, you will see that all these purposes can be woven together to make a beautiful tapestry for the benefit of individual human beings and humanity as a whole.

A Sense of Purpose

If we are not clear about our purpose, we can often get sidetracked by what seem to be more important requirements. It is putting the purpose first that leads to success. The artist Kit Williams created exquisite paintings for his treasure trail book *Masquerade*. The pictures took many hours of work and were full of tiny details requiring total focus. While he worked on them, he lived in a caravan (minimum housework) and subsisted on Mars bars (no cooking). Like many gifted people, Kit Williams allowed his purpose to dictate his lifestyle. When *Masquerade* was published in 1984, it sold millions of copies.

Another young man who was totally driven by his purpose was the author Colin Wilson. In the 1950s he knew he had a great book to write but hadn't the time while doing an ordinary job in order to pay the rent. He had not been to University, so was unable to get work in a publishing company, as many hopeful authors do. For several years he had been doing menial and tiring jobs in factories or cafés. Colin reached a point where he felt that without more time he would never get his masterpiece written. He saved up and bought a tent and a bicycle. He parked his tent on Hampstead Heath and everyday he cycled to the British Library to write his book. He had enough savings to buy food from a roadside café each morning.

This lifestyle meant he had no financial or domestic distractions while he was writing *The Outsider*, which was to become a best-seller. At the time, the British Library Reading Room superintendent was the well-known novelist Angus Wilson, who read his manuscript and passed it on to a publisher. Colin Wilson was catapulted to fame and became the delight of the 1950s' media as an 'Angry Young Man'.

Obviously, it is not essential to live rough on Hampstead Heath to fulfil your purpose but it seems clear that your dedication to your purpose, demonstrated by your willingness to give up a certain amount of comfort, will be rewarded. In addition, Colin Wilson's story is a good illustration of how our commitment to bring our purpose into the world is often supported by mysterious forces – Colin met just the right person to help him, at just the right time. But he would never have met Angus Wilson if he had not taken the leap of faith and lived in a tent on Hampstead Heath.

Purpose and Intention

People tend to think that purpose requires us to maintain constant, pushy activities, never letting up, but always staying on the case. It is true that we need to keep our focus but, when we are in touch with our own Divine purpose, we are connected to that mysterious source of energy that maintains creation and, to a great extent, we can allow that to carry us. If we intend to go in a certain direction, we have to face that direction and start moving towards it – everything we do has to be focused on the intention. But then a kind of magic begins and we find events and people turn up just when we need them. One key to this is self-belief and we will be looking at ways to encourage this later in the course.

The most powerful tool we have is to visualise ourselves being and doing exactly what we have dreamed of. I knew a lovely young couple who were planning to marry and had a dream of living on a houseboat on the river. They both worked as graphic designers for the same company and every day at lunchtime they would walk beside the river and look at the boats. Sarah used to take a sketch pad with her and she painted a watercolour of one of the boats called *The Dragonfly*. Eventually they had sorted out enough funds to start looking for a boat to buy, and guess which one came up on the market, just at the right time? *The Dragonfly*, of course. Sarah had not painted it because she especially wanted that particular boat, but because she loved boats in general, so the way the dream unfolded into reality was quite a surprise to her.

A recent example in my own life happened when I moved into a new flat and realised that a number of significant features exactly matched a visualisation I have been giving to my students for years – it is in this book, in fact. The sitting room has a comfortable sofa, with glass doors opposite, opening on to a beautiful garden and in the garden is a small gate, leading to a path . . . If you reread A 'Journey to Meet Your Guardian Angel' (page 23), you will see that this is what I describe as the starting point for your journey.

Visualising, or surrounding yourself with images of your dream life – not just material goods but what you actually want to be doing – creates a magical force field that draws you and your new way of being closer and closer together.

This Week's Session

❖ By now, I hope you will have developed your own routine for preparing your space and for creating an atmosphere that supports your weekly session.

❖ Spend a few minutes clearing and invoking protection from the archangels.

❖ Now sit comfortably, relax, close your eyes and visualise yourself going to the sacred building to meet your guardian angel. Sit beside your angel and ask inwardly:

Dear guardian angel [use his or her name if you have been given one], this week I aim to reconnect with my basic life purpose, so that I can move forward with confidence. If there is anything that will help me at this stage, please let me know, either now, or in my dreams.

❖ Sit quietly for a few moments, giving time for your guardian angel to respond. Describe anything important in your journal.

Tasks for this Session

❖ The most important task this week is the following visualisation. As with the guardian angel journey, you may wish to prerecord this on tape.

- Make yourself comfortable in your favourite way, ensuring that you won't be disturbed. Allow your breathing to settle into a gentle rhythm.

- Take yourself to your sacred space and sit quietly. Ask your guardian angel to be present for you.
- Your guardian angel leads you by the hand towards a shining staircase on which you find yourself moving upwards until you arrive in a beautiful room with seven golden doors.
- Each door has on it the name of an archangel. One has the names of two archangels – Auriel and Sandalphon.
- Let yourself be drawn to one of the doors and watch as it opens in front of you. Your guardian angel encourages you to go through the door.
- There is a beautiful light in the room behind the door, a heavenly colour that makes you feel energised and comforted at the same time. You move into the room and the colour wraps around you. You may be able to see a face, perhaps the glimpse of wings, but the most important thing is that you feel the energy, the vibration of a great power that can support you in all that you do.
- Gradually you become aware that an archangel is calling your name. His or her voice seems to come from a long way off but you feel something being pressed into your hand. You look down and see a small scroll of parchment with your name on it. Also on the parchment is a single word, describing your soul's basic purpose – healing, transforming, creating, teaching, protecting, organising or leading.
- The voice tells you to remember your purpose and to make a commitment to it.
- The archangel may have other things to say to you and will offer you another symbolic gift that holds meaning for you, to go with your parchment. Spend a couple of minutes with this angel, who is able to remind you of your life purpose and how to manifest it.
- As you leave, with the parchment and your gift safely in your hand, your guardian angel puts a protective wing around your shoulder and guides you gently down the staircase, back to your sacred space.
- Now, sit quietly with your guardian angel for a few moments,

allowing the word on your parchment to settle into your mind.

- Now, give the parchment and your gift to your guardian angel for safekeeping. Gently come out of your meditation, stretching your limbs, and grounding yourself in the usual way.

❖ Write a report of this meeting in your journal.

❖ As soon as possible after this, take a large piece of paper and write your basic purpose in large letters at the top. Next, write down everything you do in your life that relates to this purpose, including both your daily work and your part-time activities. For example, if my basic purpose is teaching, I could include the workshops I give and the books that I write, all of which have a teaching purpose.

❖ Now write down any activities that do not seem to have anything to do with your purpose. These will fall into two categories – things like organising your daily life, travel, cooking, shopping and so on; and also things you may be doing out of force of habit that you could give up, to create more time and energy for your real purpose.

❖ When you have put down as many of your activities as you can think of, draw circles in red around the most significant and important ones. Then draw blue circles around essential daily activities and green circles around any items that could be changed.

❖ On another large piece of paper draw a big tree, with strong roots reaching downwards and leafy branches spreading upwards and out to the edges of the paper. Beneath the roots write your basic purpose in large letters. In the branches draw at least six large red circles to represent fruit. Within each fruit, write a word that represents how your purpose could manifest in the world. For example, if your purpose is creating, you could write 'painting', in one circle; 'a beautiful home' in another and so on.

❖ Again on a large sheet of paper, draw an outline to represent your head. Around this draw thought bubbles in which you can stick the cut-out pictures you have been collecting during the week.

Add anything you want to with coloured pens, representing your hopes and fantasies – don't try to be realistic, let your imagination flow freely. I call this a vision map – it is a useful process to revisit every so often. I make one at the beginning of each new year.

❖ Sitting with your sheets of paper, try to analyse how well your present lifestyle suits your basic purpose. Ask your guardian angel to be present to inspire you to make any necessary changes. Write down any insights in your journal. Pin up your picture of the tree, showing the fruit you want to grow, and your vision map, in a place where you can see them every day. Save your other pieces of paper by folding them neatly and storing them in your folder or box.

❖ Find the archangel who supports your purpose in Appendix 1 on page 206. Read the information there and write out the invocation in your journal and again on a piece of special paper, which you can put by your bed, or somewhere where you can read it easily every day.

❖ Now, read the following tasks for the week ahead.

Tasks for the Week

❖ Every day this week stand in front of the mirror in the morning and say the following: MY NAME IS . . . MY PURPOSE IN LIFE IS TO . . . AND EVERY DAY I AM DISCOVERING HOW TO MANIFEST MY PURPOSE IN THE WORLD.

❖ Every day this week read your invocation to the archangel out loud to yourself before going to bed.

❖ Keep a notebook with you all the time. Observe your thoughts and notice whether you are reacting in a new way to your existing lifestyle. Are you getting more pleasure from some of the things you do? Or are you feeling more frustrated, because you know that you could be using your time in a more effective way?

Summary

The exercises this week may bring up some surprises or they may confirm what you already knew. Either way, you can now feel confident that you have searched into your own inner wisdom and unearthed the most important piece of information you need: you have identified your basic drive. This does not necessarily mean that you know what to do next (we will be looking at this in Week 6) but it should give you an 'aha!' moment, because it will explain your responses to events in your life. It will explain why you feel good about some of the things you do and dissatisfied with others. Perhaps you will recognise a gut response of frustration or anger when you give your time to something that is not in keeping with your basic purpose. Obviously, we all have to spend time on the basic chores, although you may notice that very focused people manage to offload boring tasks on to others, or minimise them in creative ways.

Both Kit Williams and Colin Wilson were driven by a strong sense of purpose and an intense desire to bring that purpose to fruition. The passion to fulfil your purpose is fuelled by your spirit, which is represented by the element of fire. Spirit is formless and needs shaping in order to realise itself. But in order to manifest in the world it has to move through three more stages, represented by the other elements of air, water and earth. We use our minds and our thoughts – represented by air – to shape our lives. It is while we are working with the air element that we make decisions about where our passion can be best directed to serve our purpose. After this week's work I hope you will begin to see how your own life has been shaped so far and how you can make new decisions based on your sense of purpose.

CLOSING DOWN
It is especially important this week to make sure you are feeling well and truly grounded, as you have been doing some very powerful work in the upper realms. As usual, sit quietly with your guardian

---

angel. Ask for a sign to come to you before the next session, in the form of a dream, an event, or perhaps a book. Do the daily tasks that have been set and talk about your experiences to anyone who will listen. You will be surprised how many people will be fascinated by your process and may want to join the course as well.

Week 6

Making New Plans

We can do anything we want to do if we stick to it
long enough.
HELEN KELLER

The aim this week is to consolidate the insights you have gathered
so far and to create a plan that clears the way for the future. Now
you have a clearer idea of your fundamental purpose you can identify the finer strands of your individual destiny and find your way
to be in the world. If your purpose is to teach, what kind of teaching
calls you? School teaching? Adult education? Do you have a particular subject in mind? If you are a born healer, do you want to work
with humans or animals? Do you want to go into conventional or
holistic medicine? Or have you a gift for spiritual healing?

I am not just talking about career choices but how you live your
life overall. Some purposes may not lead to paid employment. If
your role is to protect, you could be a policeman or a mother, and
no one offers a salary to mothers. You may need to find a way of
paying the rent while you develop your purpose on the side, like
the poet who took a job as a lock-keeper: he had a house that went
with the job, money for his keep and plenty of time to write poems
in between the coming and going of boats.

You must not assume that creating your destiny will be difficult.
When you start to flow with the essential design of your own life,
things gradually begin to happen effortlessly. When people have a

tough time getting their lives on track, I suggest – from personal experience – the reason the way seems hard is because they are struggling against social or family expectations. In Week 7 you will be getting some help with this when we take a look at the 'gremlins', who represent your inner fears and anxieties. In the meantime, your task is to assess the true direction for your life and set your compass accordingly.

This week's process is not primarily about setting goals, although you will be making some choices that will realign you and allow you to assess what changes you need to initiate. What you will be doing is opening the way for these changes to unfold as naturally as a rose unfolds petals from its bud. Remember that for a human being this unfolding can never happen too late. Latent beauty, gifts and talents can always be awakened – one lovely example is the writer Mary Wesley, who was 70 when her first book was published. She went on to be a highly successful writer, with her stories made into films and television series; her last book was published the year before she died at the age of 90. In an interview shortly before she died, she said: 'I have no patience with people who grow old at 60 just because they are entitled to a bus pass. Sixty should be the time to start something new, not put your feet up.'

Another favourite story of mine is about an inspiring woman called Asphodel P. Long, who worked as a business press journalist. When she retired Asphodel went to London University, gained an Honours degree in Theology and spent the next 20 years researching and studying the feminine aspect of the Divine. She travelled throughout Britain, Europe and the USA, giving lectures and workshops.

One of the things you may start to notice as you work through this course is that people around you – friends, family and workmates – will sense that you are changing and will make observations, perhaps not always kind ones. If you have been a dahlia in a bed of other dahlias and you start to develop pansylike qualities, the dahlias will be quick to spot the difference. I chose a pansy because I want to illustrate that the new flower you are becoming is not necessarily better or grander than the other flowers. (Of course, you may be a sunflower, which would certainly overshadow the dahlias.) The true glory of a flower in a garden is not that it is any more wonderful than any of the other plants but that it has grown straight and true to its potential. Some of your friends may start to realise that perhaps they have also put down their roots in the wrong flowerbed; if they cannot see a way to change they may get jealous. You could always suggest they try doing this course!

On a more positive note, you may also begin to realise that your growing relationship with your guardian angel is paying real dividends. You will notice more and more things coming into your life that are helpful and supportive, in the shape of new people, information and opportunities. Always acknowledge these and say thank you. In the Jewish tradition there is a phrase for acknowledging good things that I find really useful: *Baruch attah Adonai*, which means 'Blessed is the Eternal One', followed by whatever is appropriate. For example, while writing this I am sitting in a flower-filled garden with my pretty white cat Cleo lying in the sunshine. So when I look up and feel thankful that I can be doing what I enjoy in beautiful surroundings, I say: 'Blessed is the Eternal One for beautiful gardens, pussy cats and laptops.' I also use this phrase if I am feeling down, to remind myself how fortunate I am. I am sure you can find a phrase that will suit you, to remind yourself how good things are and to acknowledge the new things that are coming into your life.

The Best-laid Plans

Steve had been working as a graphic designer for many years but wanted to develop his musical interests. His wife, Maggie, was expanding her holistic therapy business and needed office space; she also wanted Steve to help her create some relaxation and meditation CDs for her clients. Near their home was an old church, converted into studios, where some celebrated musicians had started their careers and Steve had a dream of getting a studio there himself. Meanwhile, he agreed on a compromise: Maggie and he could rent an office together, with enough space to section off part of it as a small studio. He worked hard on a business plan, giving himself a few headaches as he wrestled with figures for the cash flow so that they could apply for a bank loan.

Maggie and Steve decided it would be prudent to start with a small office for Maggie and to use some of the bank loan to hire studio space for her first CD. By a nice 'coincidence', their neighbour, also a musician, put them in touch with Mark, who owned a studio nearby. Maggie and Steve spent a couple of days recording and through this learned that Mark's brother, Patrick, had a studio in the old church.

After a few months, Maggie's business was not lifting off as quickly as they had hoped and Steve felt that his plan for getting a studio via Maggie's project was going pear-shaped. Maggie was not very happy either, especially because Steve had accumulated lots of music kit which was filling up their spare room. One day they had a heated exchange about the best way forward. Maggie told Steve that although she valued all his work, he had to find some other way to get his music going and Steve was getting angry because he could not see why his sensible plan was not being supported by the universe. In the middle of this lively debate the telephone rang. It was Mark's brother Patrick: a section of his studio in the old church was coming up for rent and would Steve be interested? So Maggie put her office back in the flat and Steve moved his kit into the old church, just as he had dreamed of.

Now, the interesting thing about this tale is that Steve did get what he wanted but not exactly in the way he thought it would happen. He had had the intention of getting a studio by supporting Maggie's project, believing her work would create enough income for him to use part of her space for his music. This did not happen. But it was because he was helping Maggie that he met Mark and Patrick, who liked him; then Patrick immediately thought of Steve when he wanted a new tenant. This is an extremely good example of how you can plan something which at first may seem not to be working but, if your intention is clear and if you persevere, your vision will succeed.

This Week's Session

❖ Prepare your room in the usual way.
❖ Now sit comfortably, relax, close your eyes and visualise yourself once more sitting beside your guardian angel in your sacred building. Ask for your angel's help:
Dear guardian angel [use his or her name if you have been given one], this week I am going to make some decisions that will help to refocus my life. Please guide me and please bring to my attention any important issues that I may have missed. If there is anything that will help me at this stage, please let me know, either now, or in my dreams.
❖ Sit quietly for a few moments, giving time for your guardian angel to respond. Remember to record anything significant in your journal.

Tasks for this Session

❖ Use an A3 (297x420mm) sheet of paper, a fat black felt pen and any coloured pens of your choice. In the middle of the page write, in block capitals MY MAIN PURPOSE IN LIFE IS TO . . . followed by the purpose that you identified in last week's tasks. Now, ask your guardian angel to be with you at your right shoulder while you sit and ponder, imagining what kind of activities could develop from this purpose. Using any colours you fancy, write down all the ideas that come into your head. Some of them may seem really obvious because you are already doing them. Some may surprise you. In this kind of work ideas can pop up from the hidden depths of your mind; most people call this process 'brainstorming', I prefer to call it 'deep-sea diving'. The mind is like an ocean, with treasures waiting to be drawn to the surface. This task should help you find a few pearls that will help to clarify your direction in life.
❖ Allow yourself 20 minutes of quiet time with your guardian angel. Go to your sacred space and ask your guardian to take you on a journey to see yourself at the very end of your life – after you have just left it, in fact. Your guardian angel will be at your side

as you look back and review your whole life from the start, through the present and the future. He or she will help you understand the ups and downs of your history and will help you envision the years ahead as though you had already lived them. The presence of your guardian will allow you to look objectively at any painful events and understand how they fit into your story.

❖ When you have completed this journey, record what happened in your journal and consider whether the future years you have imagined include what you truly want, or whether this scenario is based on what will unfold if you do not make changes now.

❖ Now, identify any changes you need to make in order for your ideal destiny to come true. How do you use your time? How many of your activities really engage you at heart level? How can you rebalance your life to include more purposeful activities? Each time you consider any life-changing possibility, ask your guardian angel to help you make a wise choice, especially if it will affect other people's lives. Make a list of the most important changes you will have to make.

❖ Identify the areas where you could develop your heartfelt desires, even if they do not produce an instant income. Remember, some people just do what they love doing, irrespective of the financial return. J.K. Rowling spent hours in an Edinburgh café, with her baby beside her in a pram, writing the first Harry Potter book. Obviously, she hoped to get published and paid. But she knew how competitive the world of publishing is and she cannot have envisaged becoming a multimillionaire – in fact, when the first book was accepted, her agent said, 'Don't give up the day job.' Today Vincent van Gogh's paintings sell for millions and are considered among the great treasures of the world of art but he could only survive through his brother Theo's handouts. The writer Jeanette Winterston has said, 'I put my success down to doing what I love best. If you love something you pour all your energy into it. Making money and being famous are by-products of success, but they shouldn't be the goal.' Perhaps you have come across the saying 'be – do – have': keep this in mind when you are making your choices.

Tasks for the Week

❖ Set yourself one specific goal and a date by which you want to see a result. Choose something small, though not necessarily easy. It is useful to think of a challenge, something that will break down your habitual way of doing things. For example, you may have identified your purpose as organising and realise that your usual way to develop this potential is in the home. Look around for a new outlet for this purpose, such as taking a group of children to the seaside in the holidays. Shape up your idea and test it out with other people who may want to get involved. It may not happen immediately but creating the vision for the activity should be a priority during this week. The idea is for you to check whether you are on the right track: if things fall into place pretty easily (obviously every project can have its glitches) and if you gain a great deal of satisfaction from it, then you will get confirmation of your purpose in life.

❖ Make some time during the week to go through the Review of Part 2 below.

REVIEW OF PART 2 – AIR
Look back at the exercises you completed in the air stage, Weeks 4, 5 and 6, then answer the following questions:

1 Do you feel supported in making new choices?
2 Have you identified your basic purpose in this life?
3 Do you feel you can make plans based on your understanding of your life purpose and feel confident that your guardian angel and your archangel are there to support you?

If the answer to 1 is no, please keep using the affirmation: THE UNIVERSE SUPPORTS ME IN CREATING A LIFE THAT I CHOOSE FOR MYSELF. If the answer to 2 is no, please repeat the visualisation on page 97. If the answer to 3 is no, spend some time in your inner sanctum, with your guardian angel, asking for support.

> Create a beautiful image of your archangel to keep beside your bed.

Summary

In order to manifest anything in the world, we must have a clear vision of what we want to achieve and a strong connection to Divine energy. A continuous awareness of your own Divine power, and of your capacity to create a life of your own choosing, provides the energy that will drive your ideas forward. You need to keep stoking the fires of your own enthusiasm and passion, in order to keep the train of destiny moving down the route you have chosen.

The most powerful way to stay in touch with your inner fire is to meditate. At least one session of meditation a day, for about 20 minutes, keeps the spiritual channel open, so that Divine energy can flow easily into your daily life. Think of meditation not just as relaxation but as an opportunity to recharge your batteries. During deep meditation, the body becomes still and calm, the mind settles down and you can easily do your 'deep-sea diving'. During this time all kinds of things will come into your mind; you may find yourself thinking about tonight's dinner, or tomorrow's timetable, but often your mind will move into a clear space in which problems can be solved and new inspirations can arise. Below is my suggestion for a simple meditation technique:

MEDITATION

I encourage my students to use a mantra for their meditation – a specific sound repeated silently within the mind. The mantra encourages your thoughts to settle into a quieter pattern and this allows your consciousness to expand. Instead of thinking about little, everyday things, you will find that you are able to listen to guidance from the depths of your own being. This will allow you to receive clear messages from your guardian angel and possibly from other guides and invisible spiritual helpers.

Mantras are usually chosen from a sacred language, such as

Sanskrit or Hebrew. Many of the sounds in these languages have helpful vibrations, which connect us to the powerful creative forces in the universe. I recommend using the word *shalom*, Hebrew for 'peace', because it has three powerful sounds in it:

Sssh – the sound of universal energy
Aah for creative intention
Ommm for manifestation

Try introducing the word *shalom* into your meditation. On the first occasion, you can say it out loud a few times, then gradually say it more quietly, until eventually you are just saying it in your head.

Sit quietly for 20 minutes and just allow the word *shalom* to come and go in your mind. Do not force it. Contrary to popular belief, you do not need to concentrate hard on the mantra. If other thoughts come into your mind, as they will, do not become anxious, just notice the other thoughts and then, when you notice that you have forgotten the mantra, go back to it. It's easy.

Your body will become still, your breathing will naturally become slower and deeper. Your thoughts will gradually quieten down and you will be filled with peace and light.

One misunderstanding about meditation is to assume that you should *not* think. It is natural for thoughts to arise in the mind and when we allow the mind a free space then we find creative thoughts, inspiration and wisdom come easily to us. These inspirations and thoughts emerge from our essential being and lead us along the path of our true destiny. If you have become stuck in a rut, having made choices based entirely on practical and economic considerations, meditation will give your guardian angel the opportunity to bring a new vision into your mind and you may soon find this inspiration confirmed by events in your outer life.

So, we can see that meditation has a twofold purpose. The first is to put you in touch with your creative intention, your inner fire. The second, in the realm of air, is to allow messages from your guardian angel to surface as inspirations and new visions for the future.

When you start to work in this way, you will gain a sense of certainty. Your confidence will begin to grow as you realise that your intentions can be processed and become manifested in the world.

CLOSING DOWN

Take your time, bringing yourself back to earth: it is important to have a clear demarcation between your time for inner exploration and your everyday life. Because you are tapping into deep parts of your psyche, it is natural that new insights will come to you during the week, as thoughts or dreams but, at the end of each session, you should close down carefully, so that you can get on with work, or family life, without being overwhelmed with too much new information. Acknowledge the help you have received from your guardian angel and send blessings to anyone you have been thinking about during your session – especially if they were part of an old problem.

Interlude

How Much Freedom Do We Have?

Man is born free, and everywhere he is in chains.
JEAN-JACQUES ROUSSEAU

One important question that has puzzled Western philosophers through the ages is, 'Do we have free will? Or is our destiny predetermined?' In ancient times people believed there were gods in the heavens and that humans were their puppets; the gods could interfere at any time, overturning the carefully made plans of the human being, and individual fate was a mystery that could only be explained by external, supernatural forces.

Most people today do not believe in these supernatural forces but they do assume that we all have to fit into a pre-existent 'reality' that limits our choices. I encourage my students to turn their thinking around and to realise that so-called 'reality' is extremely malleable and unfolds according to our thoughts. Imagine you have stepped into a flowing river; the current is already in motion but your arrival is bound to change the way it flows. You can choose to move your hands around in the water, encouraging it to flow this way or that, according to your will. Or, you could just stand there and allow the river to pull you and push you. The river is also affected by other people who are standing in the water too. Your personal freedom really depends on the choice you make: whether to engage actively with the flow of water, which represents the flow of life, or to allow the water to flow around you, occasionally bringing you a boat full of goodies and sometimes creating a wave that knocks you over.

Earlier, I mentioned the two basic human drives – the Divine or cosmic drive of our soul to live up to its highest possibility and the social drive, which encourages us to fit into the society we are born into, because this seems safe and allows us to feel acceptable. It is society that creates the chains that Rousseau talks about and we need to be conscious of these, so that we do not simply go along with what is expected of us. We need to ask ourselves, 'Am I doing this because others expect it, or because it is socially acceptable, or is it truly OK for my soul, as well as for my social self?' Often the soul is asking to break free of social chains but the personality finds it is easier to be restricted. Taking the path less travelled can be tough. It may mean being criticised or scorned by people close to you, or by society at large.

I attended a big family occasion while I was writing this book and I heard a young man say: 'I really wanted to be an actor but I thought teaching was the next best thing . . .' How often I hear similar stories, always beginning with the phrase 'I really wanted to . . .' Too many people feel they have not got real freedom to be as they choose, often because they were taught when young that 'not everyone can have what they want'. In addition, many of us are afraid of rejection or, strangely, of success. So many people settle for 'the next best thing', instead of standing up for their right to be the best – not better than others, but best as themselves.

It is true that, because there are other people also standing in the river of life, events may occur that are beyond our control. In tragic stories, unpredictable events interfere with the happiness of the hero or heroine: ships get wrecked, people miss each other by minutes, letters get lost. The story of *Romeo and Juliet* is one of the most famous examples: the young lovers both die because a messenger fails to reach Romeo with a letter explaining that Juliet is only drugged and not dead. As Robbie Burns famously wrote: 'the best laid schemes o' mice an' men / often go astray'. Sometimes tragedies occur because of human error, inefficiency or lack of communication. Sometimes larger forces seem to be at work; the disaster of the *Titanic* could have been lessened if the people who had equipped the boat had been more thoughtful but the catastrophe itself was unavoidable — icebergs and ships do sometimes collide in the ocean. Which brings us neatly back to our image in which we see ourselves as captain of our own ship of life and master of our soul. Do we have the courage to set out on the water, knowing we might have to deal with icebergs? We should not make choices based on 'what ifs'; we need to carry a vision of the land ahead that will inspire us on our journey.

Perhaps we are 'in chains' because we have lost touch with our own true nature. The chains Rousseau speaks of represent social forces and to these we can add the more personal emotional limitations that gradually tie us down over the years. We can still choose whether or not to be enslaved by these. When we see that we have created many of our own chains, through our thoughts and attitudes, we can set ourselves free of purely social considerations and listen to the call of our soul. Our guardian angel is there to maintain a golden thread between the soul and the everyday self, always seeking to remind us of our true path.

Much of our freedom lies in the choices we make when we experience events or interactions with other people. Do we react or respond as though people or events have a power over us? Or do we say, like George Bernard Shaw: 'I don't believe in circumstances. Each one of us creates our own circumstances'? Certainly we are free to choose our own *attitude* to circumstances, such as lack of money, or lack of love from parents, or a physical disability. There are plenty of inspiring stories of people imprisoned as hostages, for example, or in concentration camps, who took a firm stand to remain positive in the face of terrible deprivation and suffering and lived to tell the tale.

How much freedom can a person have in a concentration camp? When the writer and therapist Viktor Frankl was imprisoned in Auschwitz he knew that his chances of survival were small; he even calculated the odds at 28–1 against. But he still acted constructively. One of his manuscripts had been ready for publication when he was captured but had been confiscated, so he made jottings on little pieces of paper, creating notes in order to help him reconstruct his book. He also composed speeches in his head and imagined giving them to audiences after the war, so that death camps could never happen again. These activities helped him to stop worrying about his personal future; he survived to write *Man's Search for Meaning* which has sold over nine million copies. Under terrible circumstances Frankl claimed his freedom to maintain his mental integrity. Perhaps this story also tells us that if you imagine your survival, you will actually survive, despite the odds.

In Western societies we are free to make choices about many things that will affect the quality of our lives – where to live, what education to pursue, what jobs to apply for. But to make wise choices, we need a great deal of self-awareness; often, when we are still young, we can set off down a path that seems 'realistic' by social or family standards and later realise that it was not the right path for us. But we do have the freedom to change direction, to make new choices and to create new results. Modern therapies and self-development courses encourage us to take responsibility for our own lives, but going on 'success' workshops will not help if you do not understand your own deepest needs. In order truly to become self-responsible we need a real connection with our own soul's needs. Once we understand our true nature we can more easily find ways to express ourselves in the world.

Your guardian angel is always working hard to show you how you can develop your gifts and use them within society, either in the mainstream, or on the fringes. Angelic messages arrive in dreams, through people you meet, in books that fall off shelves, in a timely phone call. Are you open to the messages? And when you hear them, will you follow, or make some excuse, based on sensible arguments? In order to be truly free you must be able to follow the messages from your soul, whatever the odds stacked against you, and whatever the opinions of others.

PART 3

The World of
Nurturing – Water

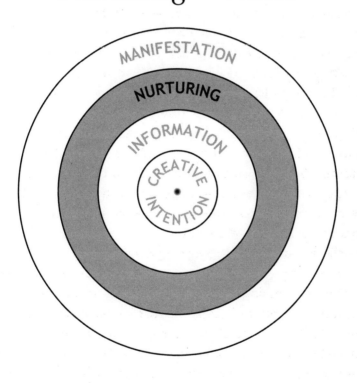

The World of
Nurturing – Water

And he shewed me a pure river of water of life, clear
as crystal . . .
BOOK OF REVELATION 22:1

In this next section you will be moving into the third element of
Water, which symbolises feelings and emotions. The word 'emotion'
itself conveys the fluid nature of feelings, which are subject to change
or motion and can be swayed by various factors, such as how we
interpret events and our interaction with other people. On the positive side, a good, healthy emotional life enables us to nurture
ourselves and others.

WATER has been used for sacred rituals throughout recorded history.
Some of the oldest images of winged spirits, which you can see in
the British Museum, are the Assyrian 'angels', who carry pails of
'lustral' water which they sprinkle with pine cones on to the king
and his courtiers, or on the sacred tree. 'Lustral' water is water that
has been sanctified in some way, probably by leaving it in moonlight or sunlight.

Water is blessed in modern Christian churches: some of this holy
water is always left near the door of the church and people dip
their fingers in it, then wet their foreheads. Even before Christian
baptism, in memory of John the Baptist's immersing Jesus in the
River Jordan, people who wanted to be 'cleansed' of their sins would

find a river, or go to a ritual bath, called a *mikvah* in Hebrew. Orthodox Jewish women still use the *mikvah* on a monthly basis, for ritual cleansing after their menstrual period.

In India, the river Ganges is a holy river, where religious men and women bathe. And in Europe, in pagan times, anywhere that a spring of water, or a well, was discovered, was considered to be sacred. After Christianity came to Europe those same springs often became associated with visions of the Virgin Mary. Lourdes is an example of a place where the Virgin appeared and people started to visit the spring for healing. In Glastonbury, Somerset, the Chalice Well is ancient but became associated with the mysterious Holy Grail, said to have caught the blood and tears of Jesus. Modern pilgrims still go and collect bottles of water to take away with them. The gardens there are wonderful (see page 221 for details). Swamps and mires represent depression and despair. In John Bunyan's classic, *The Pilgrim's Progress*, among many challenges the hero Christian confronts a giant called Despair and has to struggle out of the Slough of Despond. In Michael Ende's modern fantasy adventure *The Never Ending Story*, the young warrior Atreyu confronts a dark entity called The Nothing, whose power increases as humans lose touch with their dreams. Atreyu then crosses the Swamp of Eternal Sadness, to save his land of Phantasia before The Nothing takes over.

We often use watery images about people and their feelings – 'still waters run deep', for example. We might think of a calm lake as a symbol of an emotionally stable person. Water is susceptible to change, depending on the temperature: when it is hot it bubbles – we use the expression 'it made my blood boil'; when it is cold, still water turns to ice – we think of unfeeling people as 'icy'. In the fairy tale of *The Snow Queen* the little boy, Kay, has an icicle in his heart that has to be melted before he can love his friend Gerda. In *The Lion, the Witch and the Wardrobe,* the White Witch has kept the land of Narnia in perpetual winter, until the warm breath of Aslan, the lion, comes to bring hope and joy and the return of spring.

All the great stories about heroes and heroines overcoming trials are really telling us about the journey we have to make to reach our own treasure – our own greatest potential. These stories, and so many other fairy tales and modern fantasies, like *Lord of the Rings* and *His Dark Materials,* capture the public imagination partly because they speak to our inner hero and encourage us to face our emotional challenges, represented by the villains.

The physical trials represent the way we deal with difficulties: do we maintain hope in the face of adversity? Or do we despair and give in? In the Christian faith, the emotion of despair is often regarded as the greatest of all the sins. Wrestling with inner fears strengthens the heroic qualities that all humans have, though we are often not aware of our inner reserves until we have to call on them. Importantly, most such stories also include a supernatural helper, who offers the hero a gift or valuable advice that helps him to move forward. The magical gift represents the power of positive self-belief that is so crucial to maintaining our creative intentions. The hero still has to handle the trial alone but support is at hand so long as he or she does not lose faith.

Our emotions allow us to feel passionately about anything we love to do and help us get really involved in our quest for purpose. But they can also hinder our progress. In the world of water we need to nurture and protect the seedlings that are our hopes, dreams and wishes. Little plants need water, but over-watering can drown them; likewise, we must gain some measure of control over our emotions so that they do not overwhelm us. Fears and anxieties, doubts based on negative messages from our childhood – any of these can become blocks that inhibit the energetic growth of our true destiny.

This third stage of creation requires tender loving care, encouragement and support, and all of these depend on a positive emotional environment. This is the stage when your hopes and desires will either gain the strength to flourish, or will shrivel and retreat without budding. So for the next three weeks you will be examining your emotional life. Do you feel loved and supported by those around you? If not, you may be carrying old stuff from your childhood, when you were criticised, put down or derided. You will need to look at any negative contributions made during your childhood, from family, teachers or schoolmates, and assert your power to be free of the emotional reactions and responses that might be holding you back. But, remember – don't indulge in the blame game.

I am not asking you to deny your emotions, as this can be dangerous; if you deny your pain and suffering, you may also deny your delight and joy. As the poet Rilke said: 'If I chase away my demons I may chase away my angels too.' If you are familiar with the Tarot pack, you will know the seventh Major Arcana card, The Chariot, in which a man is driving a chariot pulled by two horses, usually one white and one black. In modern interpretations, these two horses represent positive and negative emotions, and the card's guidance tells us that we need to take charge of them so that they do not pull us from our intended path. What we are seeking is equilibrium, or emotional stability, which is represented in the Tarot pack by the eighth card, Justice, who balances objectivity and logic (air) with subjectivity and intuition (water).

During the next three weeks you will be working through some exercises that will help you to gain emotional balance. Whenever you feel held back by painful old issues, you will be able to call on you guardian angel to guide you through a process of re-evaluation, so that you can let go and move on. Your guardian is your magical helper, always on call at times of difficulty; he or she puts you in touch with the Divine power that supports you when human helpers seem thin on the ground.

During the first week's work you may shed a few tears, so be prepared with your box of tissues and your Rescue Remedy, and give yourself plenty of opportunities to talk about any really difficult experiences with someone you trust. You need to be able to look some of your old memories full in the face, taking yourself back to exactly how you felt at the time, painful though this may be. When people suffer deep depression it is as though they are stuck in a swamp, where the water cannot flow freely: having 'a good cry' can release the residue from old emotional scars and restore the flow of energy.

Now is the time to take charge of your emotional life and assert your right to choose a life that fulfils your personal destiny. In the garden of your life, you are head gardener. All your hopes and dreams need love and attention. You choose when and how to water and feed your plants, in order to encourage the best growth. If you have allowed weeds and brambles to get out of hand, or if the opinions and attitudes of those around you have been like greenfly on your roses, put on your gardening gloves and prepare for a new regime in the flowerbeds.

Week 7

Gremlin Meltdown

. . . I never thought a little girl like you would be able to
melt me and end my wicked deeds. Look out – here I go!
FRANK L. BAUM, *The Wizard of Oz*

This week's aim is to identify your emotional gremlins, those sneaky little Gollum characters who lurk in your subconscious and disempower you, by repeating negative thoughts. We all have our inner hobgoblins who whisper taunts and gibes, often repeating things we heard as a child from other children or mean-spirited adults. Do any of these ring a bell? 'Why do you think you're so special?' 'Who do you think you are?' 'What makes you think you can be a star?' Or, perhaps less malicious but equally unhelpful: 'Not everyone can get to the top.' 'You can't get everything you want.' 'You've got to be realistic.'

One of the key blocks to manifesting the life that you love, the life that you are divinely entitled to, is a lack of self-esteem. When this is the problem, invariably it is caused by our inner gremlins, ghouls and goblins who keep tripping us up or keeping us down with negative thought patterns. Our response can take different forms: we may shy away from trying to manifest our heart's desire, or we may try too hard. People with low self-esteem often over-compensate and end up over-reaching themselves. They rush around trying to fulfil tasks and obligations that could easily be carried out by other people. If you are a leader, do the leading – not the organising.

Although the gremlins are mischievous, if not downright wicked, we do need to feel some compassion for them. The gremlin mentality arises out of sadness and out of a loss of power. The children who taunt other children in the playground undoubtedly have their own problems; by choosing a more sensitive child as their scapegoat they are trying to regain a sense of their own worth. Adults who are sarcastic or critical are likely to have suffered criticism themselves. Parents, relatives and teachers often say harsh things without realising the powerful effect they can have. When one of my daughters was four years old she wore a charming pink silk frock to a wedding. She went up to an elderly uncle and said, 'Don't you think I'm pretty?' The grumpy old so-and-so replied, 'Pretty ugly, I'd say.' She was very upset and has, needless to say, never forgotten or forgiven.*

In *The Wizard of Oz*, the Wicked Witch of the West melts when Dorothy throws water over her. The old witch wore a gown that was black, a colour that so often represents negative emotions. And once Dorothy had found Toto, the little dog that seems to have been her guardian angel, she clicked her red shoes to get her heart's desire and go home. Red is the colour of the heart, of passion and of fire. We need to live by our hearts and not allow negative emotions to dilute the power of our real passion. We need to assert our own power, to create a life of our choosing, irrespective of anyone's taunts, gibes, put-downs or even reasonable advice.

One of the favourite movies in our household when the girls were small was *Labyrinth*, in which David Bowie (looking particularly handsome in a pair of tight breeches) plays the Goblin King who has stolen the heroine's baby brother. When Sarah finally gets to confront the king she makes a declaration of her own power:

---

* After I had written this story, an interesting piece of closure happened. At a big family get-together the same daughter was wearing an elegant evening dress – pink, again, as it happens. At dinner I was sitting next to the uncle in question, now a couple of decades older. He pointed to my daughter and said, 'That girl certainly knows how to dress.' I was amused by this turnaround. I recounted his comments to 'that girl' and she was delighted. One old gremlin down, I thought.

125

Through dangers untold and hardships unnumbered
I have fought my way to the castle beyond the goblin city
To take back the child that you have stolen,
For my will is as strong as yours and my kingdom is as great.
You have no power over me.

Then the king dematerialises and Sarah takes her baby brother home, to much joy and merriment from the magical creatures that have helped her on her way. My youngest daughter (now 23) still remembers this powerful statement, word for word.

The reason it can be so difficult to unpick the tangle of our emotions is that they continually affect our thoughts. If we feel pain, or distress at any level, the emotional responses, of anger, fear, sadness or despair, affect our ideas about the world and our role in it. Feelings colour our thoughts; often we cannot think clearly and make decisions that truly reflect our purpose, because our emotional issues have created watery clouds, or even rainstorms, in what should be the clear air of our mind.

A useful and powerful psychic tool is to regard the negative thoughts in your own mind as fantasy creatures and disarm them as though you are a fairy-tale hero. This method allows you to experience any problem or crisis as a story and to take command of the way the story is unfolding. It also allows you to realise that humans throughout history have always had the same old problems – this is why the fairy stories and myths were written in the first place. You are not alone. This realisation will help you give up on the 'poor old me' syndrome, as well as empower you with a mental sword as magical as King Arthur's Excalibur.

The medieval Church identified seven particular gremlins, the seven 'deadly sins'. I do not find 'sin' a helpful word at all. (It should be banished from the dictionary, like 'evil', which is one of the most dangerous words in our vocabulary.) These negative traits only present real difficulties when we allow them to become habitual. But if you think of them as characters you can converse with, then you can take power over your own gremlins and sweep them out of your inner landscape, leaving the air fresh and the water sparkling.

Most of the seven gremlins take hold when you are small, as a response to the people around you, or to particular events. All seven create blocks or barriers to your success in life. They prevent you relating to other people and sap your energy, so that you find it hard to keep your focus.

❖ *Pride* is a response to being continually put down or ridiculed, rather than encouraged. In order to maintain a sense of dignity in one's own soul, to lay claim to some self-esteem, you may have created a protective aura around you so that people find you stand-offish or arrogant.

❖ *Wrath* is a response to painful experiences. Your ego is furious that you should have been treated in this way, either by other people or by 'fate'. This anger can either be expressed outwardly, in anti-social behaviour, or covertly, when it leads to manipulation in emotional or business relationships.

❖ *Envy* lifts its ugly head when you feel left out, hard done by, and undernourished at a soul level. Part of you is always looking at the world, thinking someone else's lot must be better than your own.

❖ *Lust* is not just about the kind of intense sexual desire that arises out of a purely animal response, without being based on love and respect for the other party. It is also about yearning for material goods that seem to have some irresistible lure but which you often find, once you have acquired them, quickly lose their appeal. This is because they do not have anything to do with your real needs, physical, emotional or spiritual. 'All that glitters is not gold', the saying goes. This wanting arises because you feel something is missing from your life, usually because you are not in touch with your soul's code.

❖ *Gluttony*. Over-consuming anything that in small doses is not harmful – food, alcohol, or even tobacco and mind-expanding drugs – is a primary 'sin' in modern Western society. Again, this is a response to a sense of emptiness and the need to experience something intensely because our material lives are essentially bland. Excesses of booze and drugs take the mind out of everyday reality but they tend to cloud, rather than clarify, the spirit.

❖ *Avarice* is the tendency to spend one's energy working out how to get more money or goods. Unlike the lustful person, who can easily let go of yesterday's must-have gadget, the avaricious person hoards everything and finds it difficult to give anything away. This trait is based on fear of lack and is often based on a sense of lack in childhood.

❖ *Sloth*, or idleness, indolence, laziness. This character trait is invariably based on fear, either of failure, or of success. And this in turn is based on low self-esteem. If you failed at school, part of you may be thinking 'Why should I bother to try'? And even if you were successful once, you might not be able to meet expectations a second time around.

Have a good think about these characters. I think of them as little imps, or gargoyles, scurrying around, trying to trip us up. During this week's session you will be identifying whether any of them are keeping you in thrall.

Trisha's Gremlin Dream

Trisha, one of my students, appeared self-confident, but her 'gremlin' was an inability to stand up for herself when attacked. She told the group that she had joined the course because of a dream, in which she was living in a house – not one she knew – by a river. In the dream Trisha walked from the front door and looked into the river. She could see her own reflection but she could also see a dark shadow swimming around beneath the surface, which might have been a fish, though she could not be sure. At the same time she felt a reassuring hand on her shoulder. She couldn't see anyone but had the impression that someone who cared for her was nearby. Later, when she told a friend about the dream, her friend suggested that the invisible hand might belong to her guardian angel; hearing about my course seemed to be a nice piece of synchronicity.

When the group embarked on the subject of gremlins, Trisha had a recurrence of the same dream. In the new version, the shadowy creature became clearer; it climbed out of the river and sat by her feet, scratching and biting her. She told us that the creature looked a bit like the gargoyles which are so familiar to anyone living in Oxford. It also reminded her of a girl she was at school with when she was about ten. This girl had accused Trisha of taking her fancy pen and when Trisha had tried to react calmly and pleasantly, had literally scratched and bitten her. In this second dream the gentle hand was still on her shoulder but this time she heard a voice, telling her that even when people are difficult or nasty, she needed to remember that the higher good will always prevail. She knew that the voice came from her guardian angel. She was also told that even the spiteful girl had an angel, who was trying to help her. Trisha told the group that she felt the dream was not only about an old episode, when she had felt threatened and vulnerable, but was also telling her even gremlins have higher possibilities.

Nick's Lifeline

One of my students, Nick, had recently been divorced and was having financial problems. When he tried writing a story with himself as hero, he imagined himself in a small fishing boat trying to reach safety in a storm. He was dressed in oilskins and two of his university friends were with him. The boat was being thrown about by the gale and he kept seeing sharp, treacherous rocks. He was sure the boat would sink and was worried because he didn't know how to swim. Nick told us he didn't know how the story could end safely and we talked about how this represented his fears about life generally. For him, the rocks were like gremlins, threatening and destructive; he couldn't see how his former friends could possibly help him with his present problem – he hadn't seen them for years and, like him, they had been easy-going about money. Other members of the group suggested that he should invent a character for his story who would give him a lifeline.

The following week Nick came back with a big grin on his face. He had created a new twist to his story, in which his boat did crash on the rocks but a passing trawler spotted the three men bobbing about in their life jackets. The trawler's captain sent out a lifeboat and welcomed the sorry fishermen with rugs and hot drinks. Nick was satisfied with this idea but was amazed at what transpired next. During the following week, his bank manager called him in for an interview about his increasing overdraft – the moment Nick was dreading. But the bank manager was really helpful and suggested a way to consolidate all his credit cards and loans, in order to reduce his monthly outgoings. Nick nearly danced out of the bank. On the way home he went into a nearby newsagent's, where there just happened to be a charity box on the counter for the Royal Lifeboat Fund. Nick put a £20 note in the box, without a second thought.

This Week's Session

❖ After your usual preparation, sit comfortably, relax, close your eyes and visualise yourself going to the sacred building to meet your guardian angel. Sit beside your angel and ask inwardly:
Dear guardian angel [use his or her name if you have been given one], this week I aim to clear negative feelings, so that I can make decisions based on purpose and not on fear. Please support and protect me as I deal with my inner gremlins. Show me how to loosen their power so that I can reclaim my confidence and self-esteem. If there is anything that will help me at this stage, please let me know, either now, or in my dreams.

❖ Sit quietly for a few moments, giving time for your guardian angel to respond. Describe anything important in your journal.

Tasks for this Session

❖ Ask yourself how many of the seven mean little gremlins (the so-called 'sins') have wriggled their way into your psyche. Create little pictures of any that are giving you serious problems. Choose amusing names for these characters, for example Lazy Lizzie, or Greedy Gilbert. Creating jokes out of problems is a good policy, since humour is a powerful antidote to pain and distress. Pick out one particularly tricky character and draw a bigger image, so that you can stand it up somewhere and have a conversation with it. You can close your eyes and imagine this character, if this is easier for you. Search your memory and see if you can remember the time when this character might have started to take power. The next exercise may help with this.

❖ Look at three different stages of your younger life: when you were about five, starting primary school; when you were about 11, starting secondary school; and when you were about 16, making decisions about your future. Recall any people – teachers, family, classmates – who discouraged you at these times. Remember how you reacted. If you were sensitive you may well have kept quiet, rather than stand up for yourself.

❖ Now imagine yourself in the same situations, at the same ages, but that now your guardian angel is by your side and you are a child filled with Divine wisdom and certainty. From this new standpoint, find a different way to speak to these people. Write an account of the powerful way you deal with criticism or taunts. Draw little pictures, showing yourself as a wise child, able to reply to others who put you down.

❖ Write down the ten most significant put-downs you heard during your growing years. Next to each put-down write an assertive statement that makes you feel empowered and in control of your own destiny.

❖ Now think of something you would really like to do but are nervous or afraid of doing. Search your own mind and see if you can identify the nature of your fear. Are you afraid of other people's scorn? Are you frightened of failure? Or that you won't do it perfectly? Are you frightened you won't be able to earn enough money doing something you love? Imagine that your fear is a nasty creature, a goblin or a gremlin that is getting in your way. Draw a picture of your gremlin and write down all the mean things it is saying to you. Talk to it, telling it that you are not going to listen to any more nonsense, that you have as much right as anyone to do what you want to do and to be what you want to be. Keep your picture and if the gremlin starts yattering at you again, get the drawing out and repeat the exercise. You could make up a statement of your own power, rather like the one Sarah used in *Labyrinth;* keep repeating, 'You have no power over me.'

❖ Rule two columns on a page in your journal. In one column write down your weaknesses, in the other your strengths. Most people automatically think up a longer list of weaknesses. So take another look at your strengths and make sure you haven't missed anything. Now visualise yourself in your sacred space with your guardian angel and spend some time discussing your weaknesses and asking for help. Ask your guardian angel for a symbolic gift that has meaning for you and will help you when you are feeling in need of extra courage.

Tasks for the Week

❖ Read some stories, or watch some movies on DVD or video, in which the hero or heroine has to overcome great odds in order to get home, save someone, or find a treasure. *The Lord of the Rings* is especially good for this exercise because Frodo Baggins, the hobbit, is such an unlikely hero. Frodo often feels he is not up to the task of reaching the Mountain of Doom where he must destroy the Ring of Power but he is constantly supported by his friend Sam. A character like Sam has a very simple attitude – what has to be done, has to be done. This is called being 'dogged' and Sam is like a faithful dog, watching over Frodo through thick and thin. Guardian angels are dogged.

❖ Write a story with yourself as hero or heroine, in which you are looking for your heart's desire. See if you can think of some helpers you have really met in your life and include them. If you feel you have not had enough help and support, invent some extra characters with useful attributes, such as courage, humour, strength. Remember how the characters in *The Wizard of Oz* had real weaknesses at the beginning but developed their strengths as they were faced with challenges along the road. In your story you can write about your personal development, the wisdom you have been gaining on the way and will go on gaining in the future.

Summary

Old messages and painful episodes hang around in our subconscious like weeds at the bottom of a lake, sometimes tangling round our thoughts and pulling us down. This week's exercises have been part of a process that should help to clear some of these. At the least it will alert you to what is going on in your subconscious. When you are looking at past issues, you need to acknowledge your hurts but be careful not to feel sorry for yourself. Sadness acts as a dampener, reducing your enthusiasm and disconnecting you from your Divine thread. If you do find yourself feeling in the doldrums, make sure you talk to a supportive friend.

If you felt unsupported as a child, for whatever reason, remember that you can call on higher powers for personal support. Your guardian angel is always with you and you can also call on the archangels for help. As I mentioned in Week 5, the archangels have different roles to play; for example, Michael helps with courage, Raphael with healing, Hanael with assertiveness and so on. The angels and archangels are there for you, whatever you do. They don't criticise and they don't complain. They just keep on walking beside you however dark the forests of your life become.

We should never underestimate the power of our mind to create effects in the world. We tend to think of the world as being what surrounds us, as the place that we happen to come into. But we and the world are mutually dependent and when we envision good things not only for ourselves, but equally for everyone else, then magic starts to happen. Each one of us has a perfect right to be here, to be who we are, and to expect wonderful things for ourselves. Here is a poem of mine that encapsulates this:

Being who I am
Makes the world whole.
The world, being what it is,
Makes me whole.
How could we be,
Without each other?

As soon as Nick had invented a hopeful, positive story for himself with a good ending, he took the power away from the imaginary rocks and the wild sea and created a different outcome in his everyday life as well. Try it for yourself.

CLOSING DOWN

This week I suggest you include a bath, with wonderful aromatherapy oils, as part of your grounding and nurturing process. You have been wrestling with some of your old enemies and you can use water, essences and other remedies (see page 216) to help clear any debris they have left behind in your psyche. As usual, before the end of the session, sit quietly with your guardian angel. Ask your guardian to help you keep those gremlins from creeping back during the week to come.

Week 8

Waking Your Soul with Kisses

. . . The moment one definitely commits oneself, then 'providence' moves too. All sorts of things occur to help one that would never otherwise have occurred. A whole stream of events issue from the decision, raising in one's favour all manner of unforeseen assistance, which no man could have dreamed would come his way.
J.W. VON GOETHE

This week's aim is to identify habits and hang-ups that prevent you from fulfilling your desires. You remember the story about the gatekeeper, who forgot that there was a princess in the grand mansion just waiting to fill his life with abundance and joy? If your soul is neglected for long enough, she may well go to sleep. Then you will have to take on the role of a prince who will hack his way through the brambles and wake her with a kiss. In our story the brambles are our emotional hang-ups, the fears and anxieties that lead to bad habits such as procrastination, laziness, complaining, self-pity – all these conspire to create an impenetrable barrier, hiding our true soul's desire.

In the story of the Sleeping Beauty, the lilac fairy helps the prince by giving him a magic sword that easily clears the path for him to reach his lady love. Your guardian angel will do the same for you. As soon as you are in touch with, and acknowledge, your true soul needs, magical things start to happen: the phone rings with an unexpected offer of a studio you could use for your music or painting;

someone mentions an advertisement for a writing or song competition; a relative remembers an unclaimed endowment policy that
pays for your medical training; an aunt sends an unbirthday gift of
money that helps you buy the saxophone you have been longing
for, and so on.

Unfortunately, the reverse is also true: as long as you are treading
a path that is not in keeping with your soul's needs, the brambles
will get thicker and quite often a big bad wolf will jump out with
a nasty surprise, such as an unexpected redundancy, just when you
had taken up what seemed to be a sensible job. Or you break your
leg just as you were about to start a course that was not right for
you. (Both these examples happened to people I know.) Even a
broken leg was not a strong enough hint for a good friend of mine,
who was already a gifted artist but thought she ought to be a
teacher: she gritted her teeth and struggled off to college for a whole
term with her leg in plaster. I am still watching this particular case
with great interest – her talent is amazing and I hope that it will
eventually be realised.

Read again the quotation from Goethe at the top of this chapter.
Commitment is a fundamental magic ingredient for success in your
life. Commitment is what we need in order to get into action and
stay focused on the results we seek. So, what gets in the way of our
whole-hearted commitment to our soul's purpose? We have already
dealt with the gremlins of self-doubt; now we have to carve our
way through the brambles and creepers that represent our bad habits,
which have often developed through low self-esteem or discour-
agement.

The word 'habit' defines activities that we repeat over and over
again, until they become part of our unconscious way of being.
These can be good habits, of course, such as cleaning our teeth at
bedtime, or drinking a glass of hot water with lemon when we get
up in the morning (that's a very good habit). Or, they can be
middling sorts of habits, the kind that help you maintain a balanced
structure to your life, such as having regular bedtimes, or always
catching a bus at the same stop and greeting the same people on
your way to work. But bad habits can creep up on you and become

crutches, like smoking or having a quick tipple when you come in from work*. The worst habits are ones that we may not even notice, such as always doing things for other people instead of honouring our own needs; or never getting round to something we want to do, because we tell ourselves it is not really important. Procrastination is a sin nearly as deadly as sloth.

A 'habit' is also a kind of garment and we could say that our habits help to form the garment of our personality, the way we function in the world. The way others see us is coloured not only by what we actually wear but also by our everyday way of being. Many of us metaphorically wear old patchwork clothes, pieced together from a jumble of ideas about who we are and why we are here. We haven't taken the trouble to ask our inner princess what kind of garment she wants to wear.

In another fairy tale, the fairy godmother magically creates a ball gown for Cinderella, so that she can go to the ball, despite her difficult circumstances. This story has a deeply significant spiritual message. The godmother (Cinderella's guardian angel) brings exactly the gift that is needed, at exactly the right time, in order to bring the right people together. Cinderella is outwardly poor but her new dress allows her to move graciously and become accepted in the right circles. When you change your habits you will attract different people and you will find yourself called to different places.

Often people make excuses: they can't afford to take the time, or buy the equipment, or pay for the journey . . . 'I need to do a job I don't like,' they say, 'in order to pay the rent.' I've said these things to myself and know plenty of other people who say them. Why ever do we think that the universe, and our guardian angel, won't allow us to earn money doing what we love? After a while, it becomes a habit *not* to do exactly what we would really love to do.

Adults, with the best intentions, try to guide young children into

---

*   The Native Americans predicted that the Europeans would suffer illnesses from smoking tobacco, because they had no sense of reverence for the plant the Indians thought of as sacred. Wine, also, has been used for sacred purposes throughout the ages, athough it is now mainly used for social reasons.

habits they believe will serve them well. But, in the process, they may unintentionally do exactly the opposite. I have already mentioned my friend Patrick, whose parents always complained that he put more time into guitar playing than doing his home-work. They were trying to encourage good educational habits but Patrick was listening to his soul calling. What does a child do when his soul calls, 'Yes, yes, yes, I want more of this!' while mother says, 'No, no, no, you can't spend your time following your bliss!'? Patrick now realises that he ended up in a boring job, doing work uncon-nected to music because he was conditioned to believe that the boring stuff should be put first.

You need to identify the habits that block the path between your everyday self, living in its little house, dealing with all the everyday things (like bills, health issues and relationships) and your soul, the princess waiting patiently in your inner castle. When the path is cleared, you will see clearly and you will know exactly who you are and what you need to do with your time; all manner of things will be transformed – your health, your wealth, your love life. When you are in touch with your soul, a spiritual glow radiates from you – a glow that attracts comments and admiration, just as much as any magnificent ball gown.

Miranda's Transformation

Miranda, one of my home study students, is a gardener, doing a job that she loves, tending and nurturing plants. But other aspects of her life are not as perfect as she would like. Apart from not earning enough money to be able to take a decent holiday, she would also like to meet a companion, someone to share her inter-ests, to have fun with and to make love to. When she started the course Miranda complained that the sacred building she found when she went to meet her guardian angel seemed pretty dilapidated and was overgrown outside with thistles and ivy. During the meeting inside the building her mind had been distracted by thoughts of all the gardening work that was needed.

I asked Miranda to recall what she saw herself wearing as she walked down the country lane and into the woods where she found the sacred building. She was surprised by the question, but said, 'Just my usual old kit, jeans, T-shirt, boots — the stuff I wear most of the time.'

Then I asked Miranda to revise her guardian angel visualisation. Next time she did it, she would visualise herself at the start washing and changing and making herself attractive, as though she was going on a date with a new boyfriend. I then got an excited e-mail from her, telling me that in the new visualisation, when she had arrived at her sacred building she discovered a team of elves and fairies all bustling about, clearing the area and planting new shrubs. She had found herself able to go inside and relax while she talked to her guardian angel, without worrying about the garden outside.

I pointed out that actually taking the time to dress up, and look less like someone who was always working, might have an effect on some of the other parts of her life. Miranda took my advice to heart. She decided to give herself a weekly home pampering session and to start going to a local singles club. At the time of writing, Miranda has not met the 'man of her dreams', but she is meeting and dating, and also feeling more confident about putting up her hourly rate as a freelance gardener. Miranda has changed a significant habit, which was neglecting herself in favour of her work, and this has created a ripple effect in the rest of her life. In this case, Miranda literally changed her 'habit' and started to dress differently.

This Week's Session

❖ Take your time on your usual journey to meet your guardian angel. Sit beside your angel and ask in your heart:
Dear guardian angel [use his or her name if you have been given one], this week I aim to identify my habitual way of thinking about myself, and my habitual ways of doing things that limit my possibilities. I want to revisit occasions when people around tried to put out my light, and I want to face them and reclaim my right to shine. If there is anything that will help me at this stage, please let me know, either now, or in my dreams.

❖ Sit quietly for a few moments, giving time for your guardian angel to respond. Describe anything important in your journal.

Tasks for this Session

❖ Recall people – family, teachers, classmates – who discouraged you when you were young. In the film *Finding Neverland*, the author of *Peter Pan*, James Barrie (played by Johnny Depp) calls these people 'candle-snuffers': they try to put out your light. Remember how you reacted. If you were sensitive you probably kept quiet and tried to adjust your behaviour to fit what was acceptable. It is likely that these adjustments are still affecting your life and perhaps they are not good for you. Imagine yourself as a child filled with Divine wisdom, aware of your guardian angel by your side. You are certain of your path and answer these people, politely and firmly. Write a story about this, using little pictures with words in bubbles, like a cartoon, which show you as a wise child, able to respond to others who put you down. (If you are not confident about drawing, stick people will do.)

❖ How many unhelpful phrases can you recall, that you heard when you were younger and which still come up in your mind? They might be to do with money – 'money doesn't grow on trees' – or to do with your vision of success – 'for every winner there are nine losers'. Write down as many as you can and then consider whether these negative aphorisms are still affecting the way you act in the world.

❖ Make two columns headed HELPFUL and UNHELPFUL. Now make lists of your habits, identifying which ones seem helpful and which ones you know are getting in the way of your progress. Spend plenty of time on this task because some habits may seem to be positive when, in fact, if you turned them around you might get better results. An example might be your bedtime: the general wisdom is that regular bedtimes, not too late, are good for most people. But creative and spiritual work often gains momentum late at night or early in the morning – at times when the general social hustle and bustle of the world is quieter.

❖ Visualise yourself walking along a path with your guardian angel beside you:

> In the distance is a shining building and you are hoping to reach it. But there are various obstacles in your way, brambles, creepers, old stone walls, preventing you from getting to your destination. The obstacles all have labels, marked with your unhelpful habits. Stop by each one and identify how you can eliminate this habit from your life. Imagine yourself carrying a super-magical sword, which can cut through the obstacles, and see yourself using it to clear the path. Ask your guardian angel to make some suggestions to help you change.

❖ Now, make a list of habits that you could introduce in order to create a new 'garment' in your life. Perhaps getting up earlier, before the children, if you have a family, so that you can do some exercise, or going to bed half an hour after your partner, so that you have time to write down your thoughts for the day.

❖ Sit quietly and ask your guardian angel to make his or her presence felt. Write out a statement of your new commitments. This is rather like making New Year's resolutions, but be sure not to set your goals impossibly high. The best way to move forward into developing new habits is very gently. After all, the old habits crept up on you without you noticing. For this week set small, achievable goals. Next week, push yourself a little further. Think of yourself as an athlete, training for a big race and having to gain a little strength every day. Every week for the rest of this course, go back to this list and check your successes. If you have failed to live up to your own commitments, do not beat yourself up, just be prepared to recommit. Every time you do this, ask your guardian angel to support you and to give you a sign that things are beginning to change.

Tasks for the Week

❖ Set yourself a small task that stretches you beyond your usual comfort zone. Think of something you avoided recently, in order not to face criticism or conflict. Perhaps you will ask the boss for a rise. Or you will point out that the café table needs cleaning before you will sit and have your cup of tea. Prepare for this task by asking for extra support from the archangels. Look again at the list in Appendix 1 (page 207) and ask yourself, for example: 'Will I need help with courage?' Ask Michael to help you. 'Or will I need to be more assertive?' Ask Hanael for support. If you think the boss might use your request for a higher hourly rate to give you the sack, you may need help from Sandalphon who reminds you to trust in Divine providence.

❖ Here is a magical visualisation to do when you feel ready. You might like to do this one evening, perhaps just before going to sleep. Allow yourself plenty of time and create a special space for yourself. Sit or lie down with a soft wrap or blanket around you, to make you feel cosy and protected. In your mind, go back to the path you imagined in the earlier exercise:

> Your guardian angel is beside you, wrapping gentle wings around you. You can see the shining building and the path ahead of you is quite clear of obstacles. You approach a gateway glowing with beautiful colours and when you enter, you find yourself in a welcoming room where a gracious woman is sitting on a throne. The woman smiles at you and you know that she is overflowing with unconditional love for you. You stretch out your hands and she draws you towards her until you feel yourself melting into her embrace. There is no need for any words. Stay with her for as long as you wish.

Summary

It can be a long, hard journey, to disengage from the old habits and thoughts that obscure the real needs of your soul. Do not worry if the shift does not happen straight away. You need to train yourself to become more observant. Set up a mental checkpoint, so that you can regularly ask yourself, 'Does this activity or thought serve my soul's real purpose, either directly or indirectly?'

For example, in the process of doing this course you might realise that your real purpose is to do with some kind of teaching or communication. You know that you should be getting out and about, finding a training course that will allow you to progress. But for many years you have been tied to the house, being a mum and a housewife. You still need to honour this role, of course, but it has become a habit to just sink into the sofa when the children have gone to bed and watch the TV. Your little gremlins keep telling you that you are too tired for anything else and they encourage your habit. Now ask yourself, 'Is sitting on the sofa when the kids are in bed, watching some soap opera, or sitcom, which has been repeated goodness knows how many times, serving my soul's purpose?'

When people ask themselves this kind of question, they often experience a tingling sensation in their hands or feet, or goose pimples on their skin. This is because there is a kind of mini-battle going on inside you – the gremlins are worried. But your soul is calling. 'Hear me! Hear me!' As soon as you get off that sofa your energy will lift, I promise you. Now what can you do? You haven't got a babysitter, so you are stuck in the house. Have you got access to the Internet? Can you search for a course to do? Be determined to do something, however small, to shift from sofa habit to soul habit.

CLOSING DOWN

Before closing down, using your favourite methods (you may want to vary these from week to week), remind yourself that you are making great progress. You have been sorting out the old clutter in your mind and this is tiring, so you must look after yourself. As usual, before the end of the session, sit quietly with your guardian angel. Ask your guardian to help you keep those old weeds and brambles from growing back again. Then put your feet up and relax with something that will make you feel nurtured and comfortable – maybe a video, a magazine or a TV programme.

Week 9

Nurturing Your Magical Self

At night I open the window and ask the moon to come and
  press its face against mine.
Breathe into me . . . Breathe into me.
Close the language door and open the love window,
The moon won't use the door, only the window.
RUMI

This week's aim is to give yourself lots of TLC – tender loving care – so that you feel strong and ready for the world of action that lies ahead. The world is a very testing place for most of us. In Weeks 7 and 8 you have been doing clearing work, in order to create a crystal-clear inner mirror, from which you can reflect your radiance out into the world. For the world of action, you need to be clear and confident and, in order to keep positive and happy, it is essential to be in touch with deeper parts of your being – your soul and your higher, or magical self.

Every human being has a soul, a higher self and an everyday self, which some people call the ego. I prefer to call the higher self 'the magical self' because it can perform magic. You can think of your soul as the nucleus of your being, a spark or fragment of the pure light of the Divine and the magical self as the energy field, or halo, generated by the soul to maintain hope, joy and magic in your life. The brightness of this halo depends on constant support from your thoughts and feelings. For your soul to radiate in the world in her full glory, it is vital to maintain an inner connection to your magical self, through meditation and other spiritual work.

The diagrams below show your soul as the centre of a glowing ball, surrounded by your magical self, with your everyday self as the outer rim. In Figure 4, the everyday self is so busy running round in circles that there is no space for the inner fire to shine through. In Figure 5, the outer circuit of the everyday self is softened, with gaps here and there so that the power of the soul and the magical self have a chance to radiate through them. Your everyday self, your ego, is necessary for you to interact with others and get by in the world but it needs to be a transparent window, not a barricade.

Figure 4

Figure 5

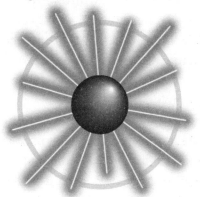

Meditation enables you to become aware of the radiant power of your magical self and, sometimes, when you are very, very still and quiet, you will have a sense of disappearing into a vast, endless ocean of light and love. This is a meeting with your own soul, who is at one with the soul of all creation, which some people call God. Regular meditation allows you to keep the path clear between your everyday self and your soul, with its magical energy field, so that your personal resource of Divine energy can be active in your life.

Unlike material energy sources, Divine energy is unlimited and everflowing. When you draw on this energy through regular meditation, the glow of your soul and your magical self shines out and, like a magnet, attracts all the good things, events and people you need in your life. If a magnet is shut away, its pull is reduced. But when you meditate regularly, your soul and your magical self, with the help of your guardian angel, are able to attract all the joy, beauty, health, wealth and happiness that you desire.

Melanie's Meditation Pays Dividends

Melanie came to my Oxford group a couple of years ago. She seemed to be depressed about life in general: she was in a dead-end job with no prospects and her love life was equally defunct. She hoped that getting in touch with her guardian angel would give her a sense of direction. During the early part of the course she mentioned that she was drawn towards drama and story-telling but didn't see how either of these could become a career for her.

When she started to take her meditation seriously some interesting developments began to unfold, quite rapidly. At first Melanie noticed that people at work were easier to get on with and often complimented her on how good she was looking. She thought she might take advantage of this and ask for a rise but when she had an interview with her boss he told her some bad news. The firm was having a hard time and he was going to have to make some cutbacks in staff. Melanie said she would consider whether to take a redundancy package or to work part time so that she would have some financial security while she looked for something else.

When she brought her story to the weekly gathering she was in a slight state of shock as she had worked for the company for five years. I suggested that she really did want that old job to go. 'Yes,' she said, 'but not the income.' However, Melanie agreed that meditation might be helping to change her life from deep inside and that perhaps the news about the job was an outer sign of this change. She also admitted that she was not quite as anxious about the future as she might have expected. She felt calmer and more open to her guardian angel helping the right new job to come to her.

I told Melanie that my daughter worked backstage as a dresser for the local theatre; perhaps she could contact the theatre and ask if they needed any more helpers. She had good news for us the following week: the theatre had hired her for a long run, with my daughter showing her the ropes in the wardrobe. But, although evenings at the theatre added up to quite a few hours a week, the income was not quite enough. 'Let's be creative now,' I suggested. 'Tell your boss you will take the redundancy – that will give you a lump sum. But ask if he would like you to do a few hours freelance for him, on a regular basis.'

This plan worked. Melanie got to work in the theatre, and earned enough, as a dresser and from her freelance work, to pay her bills. The last I heard, she had decided to get a career development loan to add to her redundancy money, so that she could do a one-year stage-management course to improve her career prospects in the theatre.

Over the last couple of weeks you will have melted a few gremlins and wrestled with some thorny brambles, so you should be feeling clearer, if a little tired. Now it is time to nurture your magical self and allow a new radiance to permeate your everyday life. Think of your everyday self as a garment: when you go out into the world your garment will get grubby and will need cleansing. Meditation is an opportunity for a spiritual wash and brush up. But more than this, every time you dip into the Divine ocean within you, you will bring more radiance back with you when you surface.

After meditating, when we come back into the world we lose some of the peace and joy that we felt in that quiet space. But the more often we visit our own depths, the stronger our connection becomes to the source of peace and joy. Gradually we become more and more radiant in the outer world. Many people feel that in order to be 'spiritual' they have to avoid the hustle and bustle of towns and cities but, once you are anchored in the Divine, you can feel at peace in Piccadilly Circus.

So this week's tasks are all very gentle, designed to encourage a sense of security and bliss. I am not saying you will never feel wobbly again but here are a few exercises to put you in a place of fun, joy and beauty and some to use as reminders when things go pear-shaped.

This Week's Session

❖ At the start of your session this week, collect together lots of magazines and any pictures you have been storing in your folder. Also choose some books containing poetry that you love, or sayings and quotations that your find encouraging. Pick out your favourite music, something that will make you feel strong and confident, not just relaxed.

❖ After your other preparations, go on your usual journey, to meet your guardian angel. Sit beside your angel and ask gently:
Dear guardian angel [use his or her name if you have been given one], this week I am going to spend time nurturing myself. Please help me to let go of anxieties and fears that prevent me completely relaxing, so that I can truly enjoy this time. If there is anything that will help me at this stage, please let me know, either now, or in my dreams.

❖ Sit quietly for a few moments, giving time for your guardian angel to respond. Describe anything important in your journal.

Tasks for this Session

❖ Think about any wonderful events and occasions from your childhood. Identify the magical times when you felt really great, such as present-giving, parties, winning a race, getting a prize, hearing music, reading books, seeing films, visits to watch football or to the theatre – anything that made you feel fantastic. Describe the feelings you recall in your journal. Create a plan to repeat the event as closely as you can during the coming week: perhaps you could have a party, reread your favourite childhood book, hire a video of an old movie, get a recording of the music you loved then. If you are on your own, ask your guardian angel to sit and enjoy the occasion with you.

❖ Make a list of activities that make you feel nurtured. Perhaps a long, lazy bubble bath or lying on the bed with a good book. Commit yourself to spending some time every day this week indulging yourself in something you don't usually allow time for. Write this commitment in your journal.

❖ Read aloud from your poetry books, or from your favourite sayings and quotations. Stand up while you are doing this and don't be nervous about speaking loudly and clearly.

❖ Dance to the music you have chosen. Enjoy the sense of being in your body. Feel your limbs stretching and become aware of being every cell in your body – your toes are you, your arms are you, your neck is you. Your whole body is an extension of your inner being. Enjoy this for as long as you wish.

❖ Now, create an affirmation for yourself, confirming that you have dealt with your gremlins and the brambles on your path. Affirm that, even if they start creeping back, which they will, you know how to spot them and you know how to sort them out. You could say something like this:

> I . . . HEREBY DECLARE THAT I AM NOT AFRAID OF INNER GREMLINS AND I KNOW HOW TO CLEAR MY NEGATIVE THOUGHT PATTERNS. I AM TAKING CHARGE OF MY THOUGHTS AND MY FEELINGS. I AM CONSTANTLY SUPPORTED BY . . . MY GUARDIAN ANGEL AND THE ARCHANGELS WILL COME TO HELP ME WHEN I CALL.

Speak your affirmation out loud, preferably looking in a mirror while you speak.

❖ Choose illustrations from your magazines, or from your picture collection, that depict objects or activities you want to bring into your life. Make a collage on a piece of paper, adding words that seem useful, such as 'more fun', 'more exercise'. Never put 'less of anything, since deep inside us the Divine is always asking for more, never less. If there is a little voice in you crying out: 'But I want less stress in my life,' change this into, 'I need more peace in my life.' By the way, although you should include things that may increase your enjoyment of life, like a new dishwasher or a Harley-Davidson, this exercise is not really about manifesting lots of goods and chattels; it is a visual reminder of what is right for you. Incidentally, both these items probably represent freedom –

from washing up, or from sitting in an office from nine to five. So what you are truly seeking is freedom, not chunks of heavy metal. Save your collage in your special folder.

❖ Now is the time to commit to regular meditation. Make this the week when you definitely start meditating for about 20 minutes at least once a day, preferably twice. And do not tell me you haven't got time – the time you give to meditation is repaid many times over because your mind and body will benefit so much. You will become mentally clearer, more alert and energetic. Write this commitment in your journal. You may wish to create a new timetable for your daily routines, so that you know you can definitely include your meditation. If you haven't already started meditating, reread the instructions on page 111.

❖ Even better, commit to a whole day when you can switch off from most of your everyday activities. I think the idea of a holy day – a day 'wholly' for you – is brilliant. You can do what you like. For example, stay in bed with a large bowl of fruit and lots of magazines, books and good music. If you have a partner, you could both stay in bed, and give each other a massage and make love whenever you feel like it. In your journal write down this commitment and make a list of all the things you want to include on this special day.

❖ After you have read the rest of this chapter, done the review and made any plans for the coming week, use this visualisation in bed before you go to sleep. (If you don't have time for it on this occasion or if you can't go straight to bed, save it for another evening.)

Your guardian angel is by your side and you are standing at the open doorway to the shining building you visited last week. The beautiful woman is there once more, beckoning you to come to her. As you move forwards you are surrounded by a host of angels with rose-coloured wings, singing the most beautiful harmonies. The angels lift you up on to a beautiful seat made of clouds and the sky around you is a soft blue, scattered with golden shafts of sunlight. Allow yourself to sink into the soft seat, as though it was a huge fluffy duvet, held at all the corners by the angels. Whenever an everyday thought comes into your mind, change it to a 'soul' thought, such as 'peace', 'shalom', 'blessed be' or 'holy, holy, holy'.

Stay with the angels and you will probably drift off to sleep.

Tasks for the Week

❖ Daily meditation.

❖ I ask you to commit to a really quiet day: even if you can't stay in bed, you could try doing less than usual. Avoid motorised transport; only walk or cycle. Leave your mobile phone at home and your handbag and watch in a drawer. (I have even covered up the kitchen clock with a teatowel on my day off.)

❖ Whenever you are feeling tired or under pressure, recall the blissful feeling of the angels and their magical duvet of love.

❖ If you have problems sleeping, after a busy day or before an important event, visualise yourself lying in a hammock made of threads of light. At every corner and on each crossing of the threads is an angel sparkling like a star. Another good bedtime recipe is the prayer to the four archangels, which you will find in Appendix 2 on page 213.

❖ Try the following exercise the next time you have to deal with something in your life that makes you feel uncertain or a bit stressed. You might find it useful when you have to return to work after a blissful day in bed, especially if you are over-worked, or have problems with your colleagues. As you set off to work, remind yourself that your guardian angel is always beside you. Visualise him or her walking along the road, beside you on the bus, walking through your workplace door. Ask your guardian angel to help you to surround yourself with a golden aura of love and peace, so that other people will feel good when you walk in and so that you will feel strong and secure in yourself. Incidentally, some people talk about creating an 'armour of light', but armour is meant to be impenetrable. So you need to be aware that your magical aura allows you to send love out, as well as preventing negativity getting through to you.

❖ Do some research in magazines, books, videos and DVDs to find material about your favourite topic. Perhaps you loved dancing and were unable to take it up when you were younger; you could find out about adult dance classes or watch the great dancers on video, or subscribe to the *Dancing Times*. Perhaps you are fascinated by wildlife: make a visit to your nearest wild life park or nature reserve. Whatever your passion, see how you can follow it.

❖ Make some time during the week to go through the Review of Part 3 below.

REVIEW OF PART 3 – WATER

Go back to the exercises you completed in the water stage, Weeks 7, 8 and 9, then answer the following questions:

1. Do you now feel strong enough to sort out your inner gremlins if they come creeping back?
2. Do you think you can observe your negative thoughts and habits, then slice through them, like a magical sword through brambles?
3. Do you trust in your guardian angel enough to relax, allowing the invisible power within you to help you create a life that you love?

If the answer to 1 is no, please look back at your story, in which you are the hero or heroine. If you do not feel this story helps you conquer your negativity, then write a new one, with some extra-large monsters in it, and create an ending in which you are triumphant.

If the answer to 2 is no, keep a notebook with you for a whole day and note down your negative thought patterns and unhelpful habits. At the end of the day, analyse what is going on and create affirmations to counterbalance them. For example, you have fallen

---

out with a colleague, who is saying spiteful things about you to other people. Your mind has become preoccupied with this and you keep turning over the same old thoughts, repeating what has been said, and what you could have said, and so on. Promise yourself that as soon as these thoughts start again you will shift your mind's attention on to something else quite different, such as remembering a beautiful garden you once visited, or imagining a kitten or puppy cuddling up to you. Always remember that you are in charge of the activities in your own mind.

If the answer to 3 is no, please repeat the visualisation on page 150.

The reason I have asked you to do this review, and to repeat exercises if necessary, is to make sure you are well prepared for the next three weeks. If the inner work is not stabilised, then the outer results will be weak. If ever you start to observe results in the outer world that are not to your liking, you always need to review what is going on inside – some of which may not be immediately obvious.

Summary

Loving and nurturing ourselves can be surprisingly difficult. Even though Jesus told us to 'love your neighbour as yourself', which implies that we all deserve love, many of us are brought up with a rather puritanical attitude that tells us always to put others first. It is one of those beautiful paradoxes in our universe that, in truth, we cannot love our neighbour *unless* we love ourselves. If you can't allow yourself to receive tender loving care, how can you give it to others? And if you feel in need of love and reassurance yourself, you are bound to resent others who seem to have what you are missing.

In the Western culture that dominates much of the world today, we tend to encourage initiative and creativity (fire) and intellect and ideas (air). But the creativity and ideas cannot become grounded on the earth plane unless they are nurtured. A seed cannot grow unless it is watered and cared for. I am sure that the reason so many people are looking for help from the angelic realms nowadays is that the angels bring with them this sense of love and gentle reassurance. Seraphim are found in the fire realm and archangels in the realm of air: they support inspiration and ideas. But the angels work in the realm of water, the world of nurturing. They heal and reconcile, they soothe our emotional wounds and move between us, encouraging us to help one another, rather than living just for ourselves. Next time a thought enters your mind, suggesting that you do something to help someone, whether friend or stranger, smile to yourself and know that you have been touched by a passing angel, looking for a human being who is prepared to act on impulse.

This chapter is probably the most important in this book, because unless you are able to nurture yourself and to allow yourself to be nurtured, all the other work will be wasted. In your self-nurturing programme, I cannot stress how important meditation is: without it you are like a plant whose roots are stuck in the surface soil among the gravel or rubble that sits on the top of the flowerbed. You need to stretch your roots down and down, into the rich compost and moist earth hidden deep below the surface. Just as you have been trained to believe that washing your body and cleaning your teeth every day are essential activities, now please accept that meditation is equally important.

Meditation nurtures your spirit and your mind, on which your physical well-being depends. If your mind suffers, the effects will eventually show in the cellular structure of your body. If you abuse your physical body, the mind becomes stressed and loses clarity of thought. Meditation, by contrast, rests the body, slowing down the metabolism so that every cell in the body is given a powerful opportunity for renewal. I have been meditating for 30 years, and people often assume that I am ten or even 15 years younger than I am; I put this down to regular meditation and a vegetarian diet. As well as taking up meditation, you could consider other aspects of your lifestyle – what you eat, your working and living environments, how you exercise. There are some books in the Recommendations on page 218 that will help you with your lifestyle check.

CLOSING DOWN

Sit quietly for a moment with your guardian angel. Imagine your-self going out and about during the week with your magical self glowing brightly. Visualise meeting and greeting people with new vitality. Now close down gently in your usual way. Send love and blessings as you blow out your candle.

Interlude

Fixing It

All nature is but art, unknown to thee;
All chance, direction, which thou canst not see;
All discord, harmony, not understood;
All partial evil, universal good;
And, spite of Pride, in erring Reason's spite.
One truth is clear, 'Whatever IS, is RIGHT.'
ALEXANDER POPE

The most important thing for you to realise during this course is that wherever you are right now is exactly where you need to be. You could not possibly have taken any other route, or made any other choices than the ones you have made, and nothing could have been different – because of who you are and because you are having to learn who you are as you go along. Learning who you are will probably mean that you have made quite a number of 'mistakes' in your life. But if you don't like where you are and want to change your life, you have total power to make the inner changes that will create new outward results. You may not feel totally powerful about this right now because many of your activities will have been based on one simple mistake: believing that you have to work hard to fix yourself and your world.

> ... *to the enlightened mind it appears as a vivid and overwhelming certainty that the universe, precisely as it is at this moment, is so*

completely right as to need no explanation or justification or fixing.
ALAN WATTS

Most human beings, most of the time, do not recognise this notion of the universe as a place which needs 'no explanation, no justification or fixing'. We want, desperately, to explain it and, even more desperately, to fix what we perceive to be wrong. One aspect of 'the human condition' is the nagging feeling that there is a magic answer to life, the universe and everything, and that, if we only work hard enough, we will find the answer and live happily ever after. In a way, we are right: there *is* a magic answer but it is a simple and easy one which requires no hard work at all. It is to be ourselves, warts and all, not pushing against the river of life, but flowing with it, up with the up currents and down with the down currents, recognising the beauty of every one of our God-given moments on this planet.

Joy and woe are woven fine
A clothing for the soul divine.
Under every grief and pine
Runs a joy with silken twine.
WILLIAM BLAKE

You may have chosen to do this course because you felt something in your own life needed fixing. If this is the case for you, I want to remind you of my earlier story of the gatekeeper, who has forgotten the princess in the mansion. The gatekeeper thinks he needs to fix everything. What a great deal of hard work he is giving himself. But if he simply realigns himself with the love and support of the princess, he will see that he could give up rushing around trying to fix things.

Once, when I was busy tidying up, trying to make my house perfect, I had one of those thoughts that seem to come from outside: 'Only the dead are perfect.' These words inspired me to stop hoovering and write a poem instead. We cannot have perfection and be alive. But if your inner world is in true alignment with your soul, then you will experience your outer world as absolutely perfect and you will be aware that things are unfolding exactly as they should. There is no difficulty with money, or in human relationships, or health, no wicked dictator or murderer, that is not part of the glorious tapestry of life that is being woven by our collective desires, by our passions, our thoughts and our emotions. This tapestry is an outward expression of our collective inner harmony or disharmony.

We live in a world of flux and change. Our world cannot exist without opposites – ups and downs, black and white, light and dark. Rejecting what we consider to be 'bad' only intensifies negativity. What we need to do is to allow the opposites to complement each other rather than pulling against each other. In a crisis, whether domestic or political, we need to take the heat out of the situation. Uncontrolled passions, emotions and thoughts all lead to a kind of hyperactivity in which extreme behaviour can erupt, causing soap-opera-style dramas that make everyone miserable.

When you open the channel to your soul and allow your guardian angel to assist you, then things that looked as though they needed fixing seem to transform themselves. What appeared to be a drain becomes an asset, a negative event leads on to something much more creative. So many people looking for a spiritual life talk as though being human is a lesser state; some even suggest they have come from some other place in the universe – Sirius, the Pleiades, the planet Mars perhaps. Some talk of being 'earth angels', who have taken human shape in order to help us out. These notions have developed from a long-standing Western concept that spirit is somehow imprisoned in the material world.

I would like you to think about this relationship between spirit and matter in a different way: think of it as a love affair, in which spirit is enjoying itself, playing with materiality as a delightful game. We only experience the world as a prison that we want to escape from when we have lost touch with our own Divine centre. When we function as cosmic beings, drawing on the power of the Divine worlds within us, then any world, any planet, any star can be our home, although Planet Earth is a very special one. And humans play a much more significant role in the development of consciousness than the angels do. Angels have no free will, so please don't aspire to be an angel. Stretch yourself into being a wonderful human being and enjoy it.

Before you move on to the final section of this course, commit yourself with great seriousness to being here and to exploring your own capacity to create wonders for yourself and for other people. Then, leave the seriousness behind you and tread lightly as you begin to watch the wonders unfold effortlessly before you. Have you seen the film *The Cat in the Hat*? In this Dr Seuss story, a wacky cat visits two children left on their own at home. The cat has a barometer which measures the children's attitudes: it shows that the little girl is a full-on control freak and the little boy is a top-notch rule breaker. Then two mysterious 'Things' arrive, little elfin-like creatures who turn the place upside down and create total havoc. There seems no possibility of putting things straight before Mother arrives but when the children change their attitudes all the chaos is magically reversed. So don't try to control everything, but do take responsibility for your actions and your attitudes. And have fun as well. Take delight and pleasure in what you do. Do a little dance, and sing, 'All you need is love, yeah, yeah, yeah!'

PART 4

The World of
Manifestation – Earth

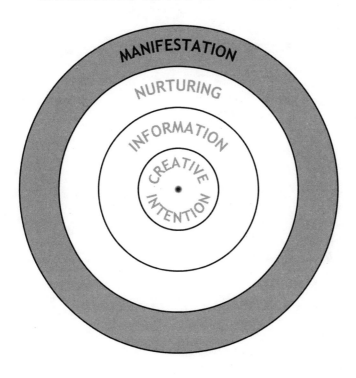

The World of
Manifestation – Earth

*Even if the world outside disappeared, any one of us would
be able to recreate it, because mountains and rivers, trees
and leaves, roots and flowers, and all the forms that dwell
in the world are pre-formed in us; they proceed from the
soul, whose existence is eternal, and gives itself to us, above
all as the will to love and the power to create – a will and
a power that long for fulfilment.*
HERMAN HESSE

The fourth world of Earth is where our inner world emerges into the everyday world. Here, we move into action, set our goals, identify specific, measurable results and manifest our visions. All this can be done effectively only if you are clear inwardly, if you know for certain what you want and where you are going. If you think of your outer world as an exact mirror of your inner being, then you can understand how you need to preserve your inner map, in order to achieve outer results that match your creative intentions. If all your actions are in keeping with your inner impulses, then the magic becomes realised and your inner and outer world are totally in harmony.

EARTH – In Greek mythology the goddess of Earth is Gaia. She gave birth to the giants who, buried deep in caves by Zeus, create earthquakes and shake the foundations of human lives. The god Hades, known to the Romans as Pluto, lives deep in the bowels of the earth, guarding the treasures – minerals like gold and silver and jewels such as diamonds, rubies and emeralds. The name Hades means 'not seen', and we rarely catch a glimpse of this immense subterranean power. Hades is so brilliant and awesome to behold that when he emerges from the underworld, he has to wear a mask to conceal his brilliance from humans. Similarly, when God speaks to Moses on the mountain, He tells Moses to hide in a crack of the rock, because a human cannot see God face to face without dying. These stories remind us of the power to be found in every atom of creation; the atom, when split, releases a light too overwhelming for us to deal with.

In the upper world, the harvest goddess Demeter brings fruit and grains for creatures to live on. The Earth can be experienced as a cornucopia of abundance, as long as we respect and honour her as a mother. The Native Americans were appalled that the white men used ploughs to till the land, which they saw as cutting open the mother's breast. Mother Earth provides our livelihood and we are her subjects. If we do not work in harmony with her, then the giants and the gods in the underworld begin to toss and turn, undermining the structures we have created to make ourselves feel secure.

As well as the nature gods and goddesses, the Earth is home to nature spirits: the elves, fairies and dwarves who are always busy working to maintain harmony and growth in the natural kingdom. When Dorothy Maclean and Eileen and Peter Caddy worked with these spirits in their garden at Findhorn, they transformed a sandy, desolate caravan site into a wonderful garden. They were growing such extraordinary plants in such poor quality soil (40lb cabbages were reported) that the Soil Association was mystified. The natural world responds to our love and to our care, and the wounds and diseases of all the creatures on our planet, including ourselves, respond in the same way. Never underestimate the power you have to manifest results in the physical world.

Our inner worlds ripple outward from our soul at the centre. The first three worlds together are constantly generating an energy field which acts like a magnet that attracts or repels the things we wish for. Sometimes it is hard to believe that we wished for what we've got. This is because we can only be partly aware of the way our passions, thoughts and emotions contribute to the world we inhabit and therefore some of our energy is misused at a subtle level, creating results we don't feel good about. Manifesting a life that is congruent with our inner hopes and wishes requires discipline and self-awareness. We don't want those little gremlins gathering when we are not looking; or those wild brambles to gain ground again. The more aware we become of our own real needs, independently of what others think we need, the more we are able to focus our energy and create a wonderful life. Then we can look around our world and say, like God on the sixth day, that it is good.

Although our outer world seems vast, what is actually manifested at a material level is, according to ancient mystical tradition, only one per cent of reality. The other 99 per cent of existence consists of the invisible creative energy that drives everyday events, relationships, health and material possessions. Ideally, this hidden power can be like the foundation of a house, entirely supportive. But there is a danger of the invisible worlds being more like the bulk of an iceberg under water. Our thoughts and our emotional life function below the surface and, if not carefully monitored, can prove as dangerous as the hidden iceberg to a passing ship. If you do not understand and confront the contents of your inner worlds, they may attract problems and difficulties into your life. Then you will be obliged to ask some searching questions about yourself, your thoughts and your feelings. What we think of as 'fate' is simply an outer manifestation of an inner state of being, positive or negative.

You could also think of your inner life as the roots of a tree, and the branches and blossoms as the outer manifestation of what is happening below the surface. If the roots are well fed and well anchored into good earth, the tree produces healthy leaves, flowers and fruit. If there are grubs and slugs eating away at your roots, then your tree will not flourish and produce an abundance of goodness for the benefit of yourself and everyone around you.

We humans need inspiration and vision (fire), ideas and organisation (air) and emotional confidence (water) in order to propel us into action and create results in the outer world (Earth). So before you proceed to the last part of your four-stage journey, here is a checklist for you, so that you can review the stages you have covered so far and, if necessary, revisit any issues that are still troublesome. Is Auntie Dot's critical voice still ringing in your ears from your teenage years? Can you put her in her place? Does Mum's attitude to work and play (more of the first and less of the second) echo in your own life, so that you don't know when to stop hoovering and write a poem? Are you still nervous about speaking in public because a schoolteacher glared at you when you stood up to read in class?

FIRE: Are you in touch with your soul's passion? Are you fired up and ready to go – to create a life that is full of love and enthusiasm? Not a brief candle, but a flaming torch.

Choose a number between 1 (high) and 10 (low) to describe the sense of power you feel when you answer this question. If you don't get as high as 5, use this affirmation:

THE FIRE WITHIN MY HEART BURNS WITH THE POWER OF DIVINE LOVE. I LOVE MY LIFE AND EVERYDAY I AM FILLED WITH THE ENTHUSIASM AND ENERGY I NEED TO CARRY OUT MY SOUL'S PURPOSE.

AIR: Have you mapped out your ideas for your soul's direction? Are you changing or fine-tuning your everyday life so that you can find time to develop any new plans?

Choose a number between 1 (high) and 10 (low) to describe the sense of clarity you feel when you answer this question. If you don't get as high as 5, use this affirmation:

MY MIND IS AS CLEAR AS THE AIR ON A BRIGHT SUMMER'S DAY, UNRUFFLED BY WINDS AND BREEZES. I KNOW WITH GREAT CERTAINTY THAT I CAN MAKE THE POWERFUL CHOICES THAT WILL SUPPORT MY SOUL'S PURPOSE.

WATER: Do you feel loved by the Divine power that works within you and supported by the angels, as well as your guardian angel?

Choose a number between 1 (high) and 10 (low) to describe the sense of confidence you feel when you answer this question. If you don't get as high as 5, use this affirmation:

MY HEART IS FILLED WITH LOVE TO GIVE. I HAVE FAITH AND CONFIDENCE IN WHAT I AM DOING. I AM OPEN TO RECEIVING LOVE AND SUPPORT FROM MY GUARDIAN ANGEL AND FROM ALL THE THOUSANDS OF ANGELS WHO WILL NURTURE MY SOUL WHILE I AM BRINGING MY PURPOSE INTO THE WORLD.

Now the preparations have been made, let us begin the magic!

Week 10

Getting Down to Work

Renew thyself completely each day; do it again, and again,
and for ever again.
CHINESE SAYING

This week's aim is to identify the activities that are in keeping with your basic purpose in life. You will be making crucial steps towards bringing your inner hopes and dreams into reality. Now is the time for the invisible processes of your soul, mind and heart to begin to emerge in the world, like new shoots emerging from the darkness of winter.

In Week 5 you identified one basic purpose from a short list of possibilities. This purpose provides you with a foundation on which to develop a secondary list of possibilities. These in turn will help you to choose the activities that create results. Always remember that you are making the choices for yourself and that they need to resonate with your inner being, which is why getting advice from other people may not always be a good idea. I have been married for 30 years to Will; we have a relationship built on soul connection, humour, companionship, good communication and lots of love. When we met, Will was 18 and I was 30 and if we had asked for advice about getting married from anyone at all they would have definitely discouraged us, or at least suggested we wait. But we both knew in our souls that this relationship was right for us, so we married. Criticism rained down but here we are, still together.

Obviously, getting advice about practical decisions, such as asking an experienced driver to look at a second-hand car before you buy, is a different matter. But when it comes to soul choices, you need to know your own heart. Then ask advice from people who seem to be on a similar path, who may be able to suggest routes to manifesting your soul's intentions. As I have already said, discovering your soul's purpose may involve trying out various paths that may turn out to be wrong for you, as in Alicia's story on page 171. Sometimes a process of elimination is the most effective route to self-discovery, even if it is a long and arduous one.

Any basic purpose will produce many layers of possibilities. In one lifetime some people will experiment with several different activities in the process of discovering the one that suits them best. William Morris (1834–96) is perhaps best known for his legacy of beautiful textiles and wallpapers, so we might think that his main purpose in life was creative and artistic. But Morris's real drive was to promote social change; in his younger days he printed Socialist tracts. He wanted to help transform society and created craft workshops to provide satisfying work for working-class people and to bring beauty into their homes. At one time Morris also wrote poetry and he turned down the highly regarded post of Poet Laureate – I suspect because he did not see how poetry could help the poor to improve their lives. I think William Morris was a transformer, who used his artistic gifts to serve that purpose.

Kathleen Raine (1908–2003) is another example of someone whose basic purpose led to an artistic product. She is known as a remarkable spiritual poet but Raine did not think of herself primarily as a poet. She herself said that her poetry was a by-product of her spiritual quest, which included the study of William Blake. She felt her most important work was academic, not poetic. Kathleen Raine's purpose was teaching, using her poetry to communicate her spiritual insights.

Once you understand your own basic purpose and feel firmly anchored in it, you can make choices based on it. Look at Figure 6 below, which shows a series of possibilities developing stage by stage out of one basic purpose:

Figure 6

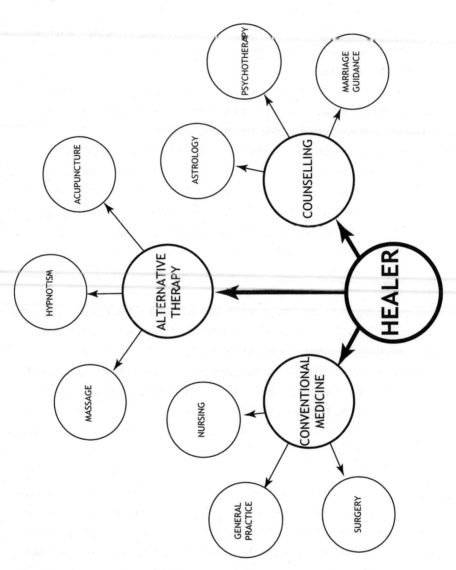

Here are some examples of occupations relating to the seven basic purposes that have come up in sessions with students. You will see that some crop up under more than one heading:

The creator – creates from the imagination: could be an artist, a composer, a bricklayer, a cook, a software programmer, a scientist, a gardener.

The protector – nurtures and protects: could be a farmer, a gardener, a parent, a cab driver, a soldier, a manager, a foreman, a banker, a security guard.

The healer – heals and restores: could be a nurse, a masseur, a therapist, a doctor, a picture restorer, a cleaner.

The transformer – transforms feelings, ideas and objects: could be an actor, a dancer, an artist, an inventor, a musician, a social reformer, a philosopher, an interior decorator.

The teacher – teaches and illuminates: could be a schoolteacher, a professor, a guru, a scientist, a philosopher, a writer of fiction or non-fiction.

The leader – inspires and leads: could be an explorer, a film director, an airline captain, head of a corporation, a politician, an environmental campaigner.

The organiser – creates structures and defines limits: could be a magistrate, a bouncer, a manager, a secretary, a schoolteacher, a wardrobe mistress.

Alicia's Ideal Career

When Alicia was still at school, her great ambition was to be a doctor. But when she sat her exams, her science subjects, including biology, did not come up to the kind of standard needed for entry to medical school. Instead, as she was good at English and had enjoyed acting in the school play, she went to university to study English and Drama, with the idea of becoming a teacher. However, while she was at college, Alicia had a nervous breakdown and did not complete her degree.

After she had recovered from her illness, Alicia went on to get married and had two children. As the children got older, she studied with the Open University and considered going back to university full time. But she found studying very stressful and realised that her real desire was to do some kind of healing, preferably something really practical. Alicia took a diploma in massage and started to work with private clients and with patients in hospitals. Now she is working towards a qualification in Shiatsu and finds the Eastern approach to healing the body truly inspiring. Alicia definitely feels that Western medicine would not have been the best path. Her natural inclination to help and to heal has found the perfect outlet – plenty of hands-on work, without the stress of academic exams and too much theory.

Robert Leads the Way

There were plenty of good role models in Robert's family to encourage a young man to go into the army and become an officer. His great-uncle and his grandfather had both served in the Second World War, gaining several medals. Robert's father had suffered from polio as a child and had been unable to go into the army himself but he had encouraged Robert from a young age to think of the army as his only choice for a career. As a young boy, Robert had shown good leadership qualities, especially in team games at school.

When he finished his A levels Robert found himself at a watershed. He could see himself in the role of leader but was unhappy about playing a role in the army – he felt that war was always the worst answer to a dispute. He decided to take a year out before evaluating his future and enrolled for Voluntary Service Overseas. While he was in Africa he worked with teenage boys, teaching them English and showing them how to play cricket.

On his return Robert found a plan unfolding in his mind. He wanted to work with disadvantaged youngsters and saw that he could use his leadership skills to create social projects for inner city areas. He decided to take a degree in sociology, psychology and economics. Robert's father was dismayed: he had envisioned his son as an army commander and now Robert was taking up what he thought of as 'hippy' subjects. But Robert knew he had to follow his own heart and explained to his dad that leaders are needed in many walks of life, especially in places where people are suffering. Robert is still at university and his father is still not impressed but, if Robert can maintain his convictions, I am sure that his life will unfold into something his father will be proud of. Time will tell.

This Week's Session

❖ Spend all the time you need, in order to make yourself feel protected and nurtured in your sacred space.

❖ Now sit comfortably, relax, close your eyes and visualise yourself going to the sacred building to meet your guardian angel. Sit beside your angel and ask inwardly:
Dear guardian angel [use his or her name if you have been given one], this week I am getting into action to create new possibilities, so that I can unfold my life's purpose. If there is anything that will help me at this stage, please let me know, either now, or in my dreams.

❖ Sit quietly for a few moments, giving time for your guardian angel to respond. Describe anything important in your journal.

Tasks for this Session

❖ Gather together your coloured pencils, highlighters and a large sheet of paper. In the centre of the sheet of paper write your soul's basic purpose and around it draw a red heart. Draw pencil lines outwards from the heart and write beside them words representing all the activities in your life. Include really ordinary things, like having a shower, cooking and eating, as well as your working and social activities. Now choose a colour to highlight any activities that hinder your purpose and another to highlight those that support it.

❖ Next, make a list of any activities that are currently absent from your life, or given only a minor role, but which could be really important in developing your purpose. For example, if your purpose is to heal, you may have been going on courses and reading the right books but have not allowed time in your schedule for actually doing the hands-on work.

❖ Draft a new lifestyle timetable, allowing for your existing commitments but rearranging your social or playtime so that you can use it more effectively. You could include sections labelled 'time for development' without allocating them a specific activity. When you have finished next weeks tasks (including your daily meditation) you could come back to these sections and decide how you will use them.

❖ Now draw a fair copy of your timetable and pin it up in a prominent place, to remind you of your new commitments. Whenever possible, take some action to establish your new schedule by cancelling old arrangements to create space for setting up new ones. If you already have new activities in mind, then making a definite commitment, such as signing up for an evening class, will help to bring your intention into reality. Paying money, for a class, or a book, or an advertisement, is another way to focus your energy in a new direction. But don't worry if you are not yet clear what you will be doing with the time you have created.

❖ Go back to the tree that you drew in your week 5 session, which represents your basic purpose and how your purpose could manifest in the world. Look at the activities written inside the fruit. These activities might include some you are already doing. Keep brainstorming, accepting any ideas that pop into your head even if they seem quite strange. You may think of something later, while you are travelling to work or washing up. Go back to your tree at any time and add any new ideas that occur during the week.

❖ Choose something you can do, however small, that is in keeping with your purpose but which you have not tried before. A one-off project is best for this, so that you can 'taste and see' before getting too committed. For example, if your basic purpose is teaching, think of a skill you already have that you could talk about to an interested group. Organisations like the Women's Institute and Townswomen's Guild are always looking for speakers with interesting topics. Perhaps you could give a talk about crystals or alternative therapies. Or angels! Choose a topic you know well and try out being a teacher for an evening. Or, if you want to make a bigger commitment, find out if your local school is looking for volunteers to help children with their reading.

Tasks for the Week

❖ Do a time and motion study during the week. Use seven pieces of paper, one for each day, and keep a record of the way you use your time. Be very precise about this, so that you can make a summary at the end of the week in which you can identify where you are losing valuable time. How much time has been wasted on old habits that could be given up, or delegated? Are you a poet who spends too much time washing up? Buy some paper plates! The colourful Bohemian Quentin Crisp is famous for saying, 'There's no real need to do housework . . . after four years the dust doesn't get any worse.' The journalist and critic Cyril Connolly (1903–74), wrote a book entitled *Enemies of Promise* (1938), particularly mentioning the 'pram in the hall' as an enemy of creativity. Women, especially, have tended to put aside their individual purposes for the sake of their children. Over the past few decades they have been trying to recover their sense of individual purpose but often find that so-called emancipation has simply freed them to go to work and run a family at the same time. And men, who used to expect women to run around making their meals while they went out to work, or developed their scientific or literary interests, now have to join in the washing up. Calculate how much time you can easily reclaim by changing some of your existing patterns. If you have a partner, you may need to renegotiate a division of labour.

❖ Go to your local library and do some research in the biography section. Hunt through the books and find biographies of people who you find inspiring, whose purpose seems close to your own. There will be quite a few people you haven't even heard of but you may be led to one of them, or to someone who is already a hero or heroine for you. Find quotes from these inspiring people that will support you as affirmations or statements of intent.

Choose at least one of these biographies to take home and read.

❖ Get hold of a picture of a person who inspires you and put it up on your wall. This person may be someone you know, or a famous person from one of the biographies you have been looking at. You can find pictures of most famous people on the Internet or if you can, visit the National Portrait Gallery in London which has a vast library of paintings and portraits, covering most of the famous people you can think of. Write a quotation from them and put this with their picture. My husband Will's favourite hero is Isambard Kingdom Brunel and his portrait sits on Will's desk all the time. But when we were working hard recently to get a project off the ground, we also put up a picture of Winston Churchill, with his famous motto: KBO (Keep Buggering On). This encouraged us to persevere, even when we were getting really tired. You may develop a whole gallery of famous mentors, whose life stories act as powerful models for you as you begin to turn your own life around.

❖ Get into action. Be focused on the project that you chose during the week's session and be determined to get it moving. Make phone calls, write letters, search the Internet for information and keep your mind on it. Then new ideas will pop up; and people will respond willingly because they are drawn by your enthusiasm.

❖ In the middle of this week, spend half an hour with your journal but connect with your guardian angel before you start. Look back at the exercises you have been doing over the week and ask your guardian angel to help you add anything else that you might not have thought of. Close your eyes for a few moments and see what new ideas emerge.

❖ Keep up the daily meditation.

Summary

Perhaps you are beginning to see that it is not what you do that is important so much as why you are doing it. When you realise this, you will understand that you can be purposeful in life under many different circumstances. Isambard Kingdom Brunel (1806–59) was a highly inventive Victorian civil engineer. I think he fits in to the 'transformer' category. If he had been on a desert Island he would probably have transformed natural materials into tools and shelter but he had iron, steam and manpower available, so he built tunnels, bridges, ships and railway lines.

You should be constantly aware that what happens in your life results from how you behave in the world and that this behaviour is based on how you think and feel about yourself. If your thoughts and feelings are in harmony with your soul's desire, then the result in the world will be special. In order to create a beautiful tree, with delicious fruit, you must feed the roots with good compost. Going back to the Divine source within you when you meditate provides you with the necessary RDA (required daily allowance) of cosmic Baby Bio.

Remember:

FIRE – Being inspired means being with your soul and standing
   in Divine love, which leads to
AIR – Beautiful thoughts and
WATER – Loving feelings, which in turn lead to
EARTH – Wonderful results in the world, good relationships and
   abundance.

CLOSING DOWN
At the end of your session, sit quietly with your guardian angel. Focus your mind on your intentions for the week. Imagine yourself carrying them out and imagine the people you need to help and support you coming forward. Now do your grounding exercises. At the end, say: 'I AM THE CREATIVE POWER IN MY WORLD AND I INTEND TO UNFOLD MY LIFE'S PURPOSE FOR THE BENEFIT OF MY OWN SOUL AND FOR THE BENEFIT OF THOSE AROUND ME.'

Week 11

Captain of Your Ship

I am sailing, I am sailing, home again, 'cross the sea . . .
ROD STEWART

This week's aim is to identify how you can bring your gifts out into the world. You will be checking that your life map is one that you can really commit to with energy and enthusiasm. You need to be sure that your choices are so important to you that to follow them up you would be willing to get up earlier, give up a few home comforts, possibly lose a few friends and generally be prepared to stand up and be counted. You will also be designing your plan of action, the map for your journey to the great land that is your future joy.

You need to recognise that you are the driving power behind your own life; you are the captain and the master of your soul. This means accepting personal responsibility for your life, just as the captain of a ship takes responsibility for his or her vessel, but without beating yourself up and labouring under the weight of guilt if you do not get things right first time. Calm seas, free of rocks and wild winds, never made skilful sailors, and every seasoned mariner has made many errors in a lifetime of sailing. The most respected captains, whether of ships, airplanes, businesses, or schools, are those who can admit their mistakes and handle tricky situations with a cool head. When you truly take responsibility and give up blaming others and dodging your own errors, you become a powerful person.

When you refuse to live life based on 'what-ifs', but commit yourself wholeheartedly to creating a life based on your own *conscious choices*, then your power starts to have an effect and you achieve the results you are dreaming of. I emphasise *consciousness*, because the life you are leading now is already based on your choices. If it includes unsatisfactory elements, this is because your choices have been unconscious, or perhaps only semi-conscious. You cannot hope to steer your ship successfully unless you have:

1. An idea of where you are going. You need to be clear about your basic purpose and the goals that lead to its achievement.
2. The map. Don't just keep your idea in your head. A clear vision needs to be made concrete in some way, in the form of a list or diagram, so that you can check your position against it. Writing it down, or creating some kind of visual reminder, allows you to become precise. Many successful people say they wrote down their life goals early in life. People raising funds for the repair of the church steeple create a barometer with a target marked on it, showing what they want to achieve. Businesses create cash-flow forecasts and set their sales goals, checking each week to see if they have matched their targets. Every success becomes a platform for a new opportunity, a place from which to look ahead for another horizon.
3. An understanding of navigation. The technical skills or qualifications you need will vary, depending on the route you are taking. If you want to be a musician you need to study music; if you want to be an architect, you need training; if you want to buy and sell property, you need to know how mortgages work.
4. Knowledge of the tides – that is, how to pace your own energy. This involves knowing when to press on and when to relax. It also includes both informed knowledge and an intuitive sense of the larger arena you will be working in. For example, you would study specialist newspapers and magazines in order to look for openings in your chosen area. You can visit places where you will have a good chance of getting on to the 'grapevine' – perhaps a café or networking group, where people of like mind gather together and exchange news and ideas.

5. Planning advisers. You need friends, guides and mentors who understand and support your goals and do not 'rain on your parade'.

6. An efficient crew. Depending on your goals, you may need more or fewer helpers. For example, if you are running a healing centre, you will need reliable assistants, such as a receptionist and someone to organise the laundry. Your helpers may come and go, depending on the length of your project. In a theatre, an army of skilled, behind-scenes assistants support the performers, making sure costumes and props are always in place. But when the actor moves to a new theatre, then new helpers move into place.

When a ship is sailing to a far territory, the map will show ports of call where food and fuel can be replenished. At each one the captain will look at the map, and say: 'Yes, we have travelled so far and we only have so many days to reach our next stopping place.' In the same way we can recognise stages in our lives: when we qualify, when we buy our first home, and so on. One of the traps we can fall into, though, is to base our goals on social standards. During this week, you will be looking at ways to downsize any cumbersome responsibilities in your life, freeing up your energy and time in order to steer your ship lightly with the wind.

A great captain is a combination of the pragmatic and the visionary and is able to keep an eye on the basic practicalities, such as food, shelter, clothing, while at the same time maintaining focus on the land ahead. He or she also has a number of virtues that ensure good relationships and the willing support of other people, in particular:

Integrity
Honesty
Commitment
Faith
Clarity
Compassion

Another task this week will be self-examination, when you will ask yourself how you measure up in these areas. Your ability to manifest your destiny in the world will be enhanced or diminished by your attitude to and interactions with other people.

Barbara's Lady of Dreams

Barbara decided not to draw a map or write a list but to create a picture of herself as she would like to be seen in the world. Barbara was a good artist and collected lots of decorations to add to her image. She depicted herself wearing a purple gown and a coronet made of white flowers, stuck with crystal beads. She told us that the purple represented the spiritual wisdom she wanted to bring into the world and the coronet her ability to connect into higher realms. Around her head, Barbara added symbols representing planets and the significant signs of the zodiac from her astrological chart; an angel hovered over her, with a shower of glitter coming down from heaven and dropping into the coronet.

Barbara also drew a large gold platter for her lady to carry, containing pictures of the gifts and talents she was developing. She was learning about essential oils, so she included the picture of some spikenard, a plant whose oil is regarded as precious and sacred. (It is said that this was the oil Mary Magdalene used to anoint the feet of Jesus.) Barbara was planning to train as an interfaith minister, so she added the picture of a beautiful book to represent all the holy texts she would be studying. She also put in a little reproduction of a Tarot card, the High Priestess, and the picture of a lighted candle because she wanted to bring light into the world.

The rest of the group was delighted with the result. We told Barbara that she should make herself a purple frock and a coronet and wear them when she was meditating. Barbara herself was amazed at the way the picture had developed. She was quite shy about showing it to us but agreed that she would keep it at home in her therapy room and would be open about its meaning if her clients asked her about it.

This Week's Session

❖ Are you sitting comfortably? Then begin by seeing yourself going to the sacred building to meet your guardian angel. Sit beside your angel and ask inwardly:

Dear guardian angel [use his or her name if you have been given one], help me to be honest with myself, to recognise my best qualities and my weaknesses. Support me as I work towards strengthening my sense of purpose. If there is anything that will help me at this stage, please let me know, either now, or in my dreams.

❖ Sit quietly for a few moments, giving time for your guardian angel to respond. Write down anything important in your journal.

Tasks for this Session

❖ Find an A4 (210x297mm) piece of special paper, one that has a sense of quality and importance about it, perhaps with a parchment finish, like the kind used for calligraphy, or one with printed decorations. Sit quietly with your guardian angel and think about your gifts, talents or potential. You can scribble them down on a rough piece of paper if you like, before listing them on parchment in your best handwriting. At the top of the list write:

> I [put your name here] have brought these gifts and talents into the world. (The idea is to create a beautiful reminder of the wonderfulness of you, which you can put up on a wall and look at every day; you could even frame it.)

Consider how any of these gifts and talents could serve your basic purpose.

❖ In your journal write the list out again, this time giving yourself marks out of ten for how successfully you think you are bringing each gift into the world. Are you a closet poet, like the American Emily Dickinson (1830–86)? She wrote 1,700 poems secretly; only seven were published, without her permission, before she died, but today she is regarded as a great poet. Your measure of success is *not* based on the number of people who recognise your gift but on whether the people around you recognise you for who you are and whether you feel you are acting in the world to your full capacity. You might, for instance, be successful in helping to replant a forest in a remote part of Scotland. Your basic purpose of healing, which has been applied to a desolate place, may be recognised only by the half-dozen people working with you, but that would certainly earn you full marks. (The same work could, of course, bring you international recognition, at least among people who know the value of environmental work.) It is essential to work from your soul's purpose and not with an eye to social acclaim or financial reward, above what you need, of course, for a reasonable lifestyle.

❖ Now, spend a few moments with your guardian angel, thinking about your gifts and the scores you have given them. Ask your angel for ideas and insights. Is the gift with the highest score the one that it seems most important to develop at this time and is it serving your purpose? Is the lowest scoring gift one that you have valued very much? Perhaps this gift could make a difference if it were developed and would make you feel you were making a real contribution. How can you share any of your gifts in the world, so that you can feel confident in saying: 'This is who I am, and this is what I do'?

❖ Write down any ideas that come into your head, but because you have asked for help and insight, other ideas, or opportunities, are likely to crop up quite soon. Choose the one thing on the list that seems most impossible to bring out into the world. Identify why you believe it to be impossible and see if there are any gremlins lurking behind your belief. These may be to do with self-doubt, or with social expectations. You can be seen to be 'too old' for some activities, for dancing, perhaps, or for rafting up the Euphrates in your eighties, like the travel writer Dame Freya Stark (1893–1993). Look at ways in which you could develop your gift, however unlikely. For example, you might now be in your sixties and have always dreamed of winning Wimbledon. You could decide to get as fit as possible, join the local tennis club and try to win a few tournaments. You may never win Wimbledon but you can enjoy your gift, and perhaps share it with others by encouraging the youngsters in your club. Our physical abilities are so closely allied to our mental expectations that we should never assume that we cannot achieve spectacular results. Ageing is very much to do with your state of mind, see Deepak Chopra's *Ageless Body, Timeless Mind* on page 218.

❖ Choose which single activity you would want to commit to if you could do only one thing for the rest of your life. Are you already doing this? What steps can you take to develop this gift? Is one of your excuses shortage of time? Check back on your time and motion study and get clear how you can shift the balance in your life so that you can follow your real desires. What daily chores can you rearrange or delegate? For example, as a parent, you might be surprised how much kids can do for themselves. Try moving some activities to a different time of day, so that you use early morning and noontime energy for the most important and evening times for tasks requiring less physical energy or creative input.

❖ Write down the list of qualities already mentioned: integrity, honesty, commitment, faith, clarity, compassion. Ask yourself how you measure up to each.

- *Integrity* requires that you follow through what you say you are going to do, that you keep your word.
- *Honesty* is not just a question of not stealing or lying, it is also about being truthful about who you are and what you need. Keeping your anxieties to yourself, or not admitting that you need help, are also forms of dishonesty.
- *Commitment* means being dedicated to the truth of your own being, even if involves being criticised, or becoming unpopular.
- *Faith* is a tricky one for many people. It isn't just believing in an outside power, it is being confident that your intentions will be manifested, that you have the Divine power within you to bring your soul's desires to fruition. Observe what

happens in your life and you will see plenty of evidence that this is in fact happening. Acknowledging every occasion, however small, when your desire comes true helps to reinforce your faith.

- *Clarity* is connected to honesty. We all need to be really clear in our negotiations with each other, stating what we want, what we expect, and what we can give in return.
- *Compassion* means extending your circle of love so that you can understand another person's position, even when they are behaving badly, *especially* when they are behaving badly. This does not mean putting up with bad behaviour (it is said that people can only behave in ways that other people permit). Use your clarity to make sure any difficult people in your life know how you feel. Make it clear that it is their *behaviour* you find problematic, rather than criticising the *person*.

❖ On a piece of paper write four headings:

FIRE	AIR	WATER	EARTH
My spirit	My mind	My emotions	My body

Under each heading write down the things you do on a regular basis which nurture this aspect of yourself. Is there any imbalance?

❖ Imagine the life you would like to be living in five years' time. In what way is it different from your present life? Make a list of actions you can begin taking now in order to move you in that direction.

❖ Create a beautiful wall chart illustrating the different things you want to do, places you want to visit, things you need to manifest to support your goals. You can use cut-out photographs, magazine pictures or drawings. Keep this somewhere visible and refer to it when you have conversations with your guardian angel. I find it useful to revise my chart once a year, at the beginning of the New Year.

Tasks for the Week

❖ A helpful regular exercise, especially if you are feeling in the doldrums, is to look at what you are trying to bring into the world and to ask yourself, 'Am I doing everything I can do in order to make this happen?' This question often brings up another idea of some further action you could take. But it also allows you to say, 'I am doing everything I can, and I trust in my guardian angel to help the rest fall into place.'

❖ Look out for signs and wonders: now that you are working so intensely to bring your purpose into the world, there are bound to be some unexpected opportunities. Perhaps you have noticed that your talent for creating amazing birthday cakes only gets used a couple of times a year, for family birthdays. The idea may come to you to create cakes for other people, possibly charging for them. Then, out of the blue, someone mentions a cake-making competition at the local school's summer fair, which gives you the chance to show off your talent to local parents. This may seem a minor example, but think of Paul Newman, whose talent for making salad dressing and pasta sauce has created more money than his films, all of it given to charitable causes.

❖ Make sure you do something every day, however small, that is moving you into a state of being that reflects your purpose. A phone call, some research, more exercise, anything that confirms to your soul that you are making a shift in your attitude and your habits. If your life has been unsatisfactory, it may seem to be quite an effort to shift into a new vision of yourself. But, as they say, every little counts.

❖ Keep meditating. As you close your morning meditation, just think briefly of your intentions for the day. When you do your evening meditation, start by acknowledging the good things that have come to pass.

Summary

When we create a personal map, based on our soul's desires, magical events happen to support us. If everything we are doing is congruent with the deep-felt intention to create a beautiful life for ourselves and those we love, then the natural energy of Divine love will give us all we need to fulfil this purpose. I have given you a lot of ideas this week to encourage you to develop your purpose in the world. You need to keep working at your effectiveness, especially if you embarked on this course because you felt a bit lost, or were aware that you have a purpose but didn't know how to manifest it. Keep checking yourself against the list of 'sins' on page 127. Results in the world of manifestation happen effortlessly when your soul's passion (fire) is shaped by your ideas (air) and reflected in a clear mirror (water), free of negative emotional baggage.

CLOSING DOWN

At the end of your session, sit quietly with your guardian angel. Visualise the things you have planned for the week. Repeat the affirmation from last week again, at least once: I AM THE CREATIVE POWER IN MY WORLD AND I INTEND TO UNFOLD MY LIFE'S PURPOSE FOR THE BENEFIT OF MY OWN SOUL AND FOR THE BENEFIT OF THOSE AROUND ME.

Make sure that you are well grounded before returning to everyday life.

Week 12

The Lotus Land

Nirvana is right here, before our eyes; this very place is the
Lotus Land, this very body the Buddha.
HAKUIN, ZEN MASTER

This week's aims are to review what has been done and to make
commitments for the future. You have set your compass and the
land is in sight, a land in which you can manifest your own purpose
and realise your soul's code. You have travelled a long way to get
through this course and I hope that the exercises and visualisations
have helped you to gain a clear perspective for your life.

I hope too that you have reached a stage where you are quite
sure about who you are and how this could be expressed. You may
have already had some thoughts about the way your new life will
unfold and these may include a change of career or lifestyle. But
although this process includes setting goals, a successful and happy
life is not just about achievements or meeting goals, it is about
being who you are, and doing what comes out of your essence,
your soul's code.

This is it!

Discovering your soul's code does not necessarily lead to an immediate, magical transformation. You may find you have let yourself
in for a long haul as you rearrange your life, letting go of old stuff

and shifting your attention to a new arena. And things will unfold step by step. You may have had glimpses of the real you, the person who is yearning to become fully realised. Sometimes it feels a real struggle, to keep in touch with the passion in your heart; sometimes it may feel that your inner light gets dimmed, especially when life delivers difficult events. But so long as you stay true to yourself, you will keep moving forward towards your destination. In fact, you may come to realise that your destination is already here.

In many myths, stories and religious traditions we find the idea that somewhere there is a perfect place, where we will be happy ever after. Over the Rainbow, Neverland, Shambahla, Heaven – all these are variations on this theme. I have called this chapter 'The Lotus Land' because the Zen Buddhist masters tell us that this place is not in another dimension, or beyond the grave; it is already present but we just don't realise it. The magical land that we have been sailing to is right here and now; to experience it we simply have to change our thoughts and perceptions.

When we know who we are, and exactly why we are doing what we are doing, we realise, like Dorothy in *The Wizard of Oz*, that there is no journey to be made, we are always at home – this is it. We realise that what is going on for us is a result of our own way of thinking and we can make new choices about what we do, from a place of complete freedom. Nobody is saying that everything is perfect, that every relationship will run smoothly, that every desire will be gratified, but what is certainly true is that this new perspective makes us realise that when we are committed to love, then everything becomes loveable. And when we act in love, then all our creative intentions manifest easily, magically and beautifully.

The Four Worlds

As you have been discovering along this journey with your guardian angel, your inner desire to be the best possible you is only able to manifest in the world when certain conditions prevail. And these are conditions over which you have great control. Outer conditions, such as social opportunities, have less to do with your potential success as a wonderful human being than four fundamental ingredients:

1. Awareness of your heart's desire, your true purpose   FIRE
2. Thoughtful planning   AIR
3. Emotional clarity and self esteem   WATER
4. Focused action   EARTH

The four elements represent your spirit, mind, emotions and body, and no one of these can function without the others. So, although in this course we have moved through the four worlds in stages, they exist together, at the same time, and what goes on in one world always affects the others. If you abuse the body, your emotions and your mind will suffer. If you have dark thoughts and difficult feelings, your body will suffer, and so on.

You are now working in the world of manifestation, of Earth, and the step-by-step unfolding of inner purpose into outer reality demonstrates how important it is to remain well earthed. I once heard someone say of a friend: 'She is so heavenly, she is of no earthly use.' Visions, ideas and dreams can be pleasant but, if they do not manifest as reality, then they are just inner entertainment, like a film. Most of us can dream up more possibilities than we can actually bring to completion, so we need to choose the ones we feel most passionate about and get into action. Without activity in the three-dimensional plane the visions and dreams will stay in the celestial realms. It is your task – our task collectively – to bring dreams of heaven down to earth.

Essential to this task is the third ingredient, emotional clarity. Without it you cannot move forward. However passionate you feel, however well co-ordinated your plan for the future, if you have no confidence in your true role in the world, then none of your actions will bear fruit. We can see the pain this brings when we read the stories of people with huge talent who receive no acknowledgement until after their deaths. But when you are able to honour your soul, in the certain knowledge that you are entitled to be a wonderful human being, then the wonder of you will inevitably manifest.

For this, the work you did in the third world of the emotions is crucial. Whenever your outer world is not to your liking, go back to your emotional life and clean your inner mirror. When you melt your gremlins of doubt, anxiety and fear; when you convert those seven deadly 'sins' into positive attitudes; when you slice through the thought brambles that fence you into old habits – when all these have gone, what is left? A shining, glowing, beautiful you: ready to step into a world of your own choosing.

Whenever you find events and people causing you discomfort, know that your inner being is being tested. Ask yourself: What is this teaching me? What is this reminding me of? If I allow myself to love this person even when they are being horrid to me, how will it be, for them and for me? How would I feel if I just let go of this anxiety, about my bills, about my weight? All your desires, thoughts and emotions create the ripple effect that manifests as your day-to-day reality.

When you are weighed down with negative thoughts and feelings, you cannot possibly radiate positive energy into the world, or attract it to you. And this hard work, and misery, is very, very tiring. The physical body often suffers, because our bodies exist in the fourth world of manifestation and the state of your physical body is a direct result of the information that is being generated by your inner worlds – by your thoughts and your feelings. This is why people who have locked themselves into impossible situations, when mortgages and bills mean that they have to trudge every day to jobs they hate, often have heart attacks. The physical heart represents the fire in us. If your fire has no way to express itself because your thoughts (air) and feelings (water) are smothering it, then your heart will be suffering and, in extreme cases, will call for help. It is not uncommon for people who have heart attacks to have a near-death experience. This allows them to make contact with their guardian angel and, after recovery, they are able to re-evaluate their lives and make new priorities.

Your Highest Possibilities

Developing your highest possibilities is as natural to you as growing roses is natural to a rose bush. Once your thoughts and your choices are based on emotional clarity, you do not have to try to become the greatest possible you. In fact it is more difficult not to be who you truly want to be. It is really hard work not to be a magical, gorgeous stunning you. So, although this book is called *Working with Your Guardian Angel*, do not think this is 'work' in the usual sense. It isn't hard, it is easy and gentle – perhaps we should have called it 'playing'. Working with your guardian angel is a beautiful experience, it is a kind of dancing; it is like being with a loving partner, when you are able to give and receive delight with no fears or worries. For me, this magical relationship with my guardian angel reminds me of words from the beautiful 'Song of Solomon': 'I am my beloved's, and my beloved is mine.'

So why does it feel so strange, to be in touch with this radiance and power within our own soul? Why, as the American spiritual writer, Marianne Williamson, has said, are we frightened, not of our darkness, but of our own brilliance? Over many centuries of human history we have been encouraged, mostly by religious institutions, but also by political establishments, to accept a limited vision of ourselves. We have been trained to see ourselves as social beings, subject to the rules and regulations of the time. Powerful organisations have never given permission for the mass of humankind to think freely and experience their own inner wisdom. When we take this freedom, to choose for ourselves, we discover how powerful we are, as co-creators. We realise that we can change the system, not by force and bloody revolution, but by spiritual intention charged with love.

Many great prophets and leaders have called us to discover our real, Divine selves. Often they suggest that we are asleep, that we need to wake up to who we really are and use our Divine power. And everyone can. Think of a top Fleet Street editor, a high-powered lady with a feisty reputation, who amazed her colleagues by quitting the media and going to work at Battersea Dogs' Home, soothing traumatised animals. Think of Clara, a Dutch woman in her forties who, when she was diagnosed with cancer, refused conventional medicine, left her boring job in the West Country and went to work in one of the Steiner Camphill Communities, set up as protected working environments for mentally disadvantaged adults. Think of the many stories of terminally ill people who have lived much longer than predicted after changing their lives. Inner change and outer change are two sides of the same coin: heal one pain and we find a knock-on effect – many other aspects of our lives, health, wealth and relationships, naturally set themselves to rights.

When you have discovered what your truth is – who you are and what your purpose is – then you must stand by it and not be shaken. This can be tough. Most people find it easier to adjust themselves and often lead schizophrenic sorts of lives, being one person in the work place and another outside it. People who earn their living doing what they love usually acknowledge how 'lucky' they are. But 'luck', or serendipity, favours the focused mind. All the pre-parations we have made, from the realm of fire, through the realms of air and water, have brought us to the Earth realm, where events, people and things can easily manifest to support your vision.

Western religions speak of a Day of Judgement or Atonement and this has always had really heavy connotations. But people who have had near-death experiences tell us that this judgement is not given by some old man in a white beard: after death, we have the opportunity to judge ourselves. Now, you don't have to die to ask yourself, 'Am I living up to the best that I could be? Am I living up to my own values?' We need to check all our actions in the world of manifestation against our inner desires and to set stan-dards for ourselves, values by which we measure how to act in the world, when to say 'yes' and when to say 'no'.

So check whether your lifestyle is in keeping with your own ethical values. You, and only you, can set these values for yourself. But once you have set them, you must live by them. Then you shine with integrity and clarity. Happiness is based on a sense that life has meaning and that what we do from day to day does not compro-mise our own soul's code. Anyone who feels dissatisfied with their life needs to examine how they are spending their time and measure that against their inner hopes and desires. Often an insight will emerge that will help them reset their compass and find new lands.

Let me recap. Your soul is yearning to unfold itself through your being in the world, through your thoughts, feelings and actions.

In the world of intention (fire) your heart's desires are generating a force field that requires
The world of information (air) to shape it and
The world of nurturing (water) to feed it, with gallons of self-esteem, so your heart's desires unfold themselves in
The world of manifestation, to the greater glory of the Divine energy that empowers your soul.

Remember: this is *not* difficult. It is the easiest and most natural way for our souls to behave. We just need to notice all the foolish things we do to inhibit this natural process.

This Week's Session

❖ Take your usual journey, to your sacred building to meet your guardian angel. Sit beside your angel and ask inwardly:
Dear guardian angel [use his or her name if you have been given one], this is the last week of my course, and I intend to use the things I have learned to manifest a new way of being for myself. I am using this session to consolidate my vision and what actions I need to take in order to bring my vision into the present. If there is anything that will help me at this stage, please let me know, either now, or in my dreams.
❖ Sit quietly for a few moments, giving time for your guardian angel to respond. Describe anything important in your journal.

Tasks for this Session

❖ Write a description of your life as it is at present, as though you were someone else. For example: 'Mary is a woman of 36. She is living with her husband and two children in a semi-detached house . . .' And so on.

❖ Read this description out loud to yourself. You will find that talking about yourself in the third person helps you see your own life from another perspective. Now meditate and ask your guardian angel to help you firm up your decisions about changing any aspect of your life that feels difficult. Ask your guardian angel to help you make these changes with respect for other people. During this session you may decide to call on one or more of the archangels (see Appendix 1 on page 202); for example, if you are feeling in need of courage in order to make a big leap of faith, you may need help from Michael.

❖ Write a statement that acknowledges who you are, including your positive qualities and gifts, such as being strong and resourceful, being a natural musician, being a good listener, having a good sense of humour. You could draft this in rough, before creating a beautiful notice to put on your wall. Begin with I AM . . . then fill in your name. Continue beginning each statement with I AM, and add your qualities. Don't be shy, be boastful, blow your own trumpet. 'If I am not for myself, who will be?' asked the Rabbi Hillel, a scholar living in Palestine in the first century BCE and the originator of the golden rule: 'Do not do unto others that which you would not have them do unto you.'

❖ Make a mission statement for your life. State clearly what you intend to achieve. Never use the word 'try' or 'hope'. What you intend will come about, if you are clear about what it is and maintain your confidence and certainty. In this statement add words that confirm your willingness to bring about the best for others as well as for yourself. Rabbi Hillel's next question was: 'If I am only for myself, what am I?' This task is about how you use those qualities and gifts for the best – and the best for you is naturally the best for creation, including all the other people. Begin by saying: MY PURPOSE IN LIFE IS TO . . . then continue by writing THEREFORE I WILL . . . adding a list of all the actions you are going to make in order to manifest your purpose. Read the list out loud to yourself.

❖ Now write about yourself as though you were living your new life, twelve months hence. Again, write in the third person and read what you have written aloud to yourself. Do you recognise the person you are writing about as the radiant, wonderful self that you are choosing to be?

❖ Ask yourself what do I have to do now, in order to fulfil that vision of myself in twelve months' time? Rabbi Hillel's final question was, 'If not now, when?' This is a useful question to remind yourself to get on with it. You could write it on a notice to put up on your wall. Another useful phrase you might like to put on your wall is *carpe diem* (seize the day), meaning 'Why not just get on with it.'

❖ Whenever you have made a commitment – to exercise every morning, to eat less, to meditate more often, whatever – remember the words of the philosopher William James (1842–1910): 'Suffer no exception.' That is, if you say you are going to do something, do it. Don't just do it when you feel like it; be consistent, be disciplined, be professional. Don't dodge the commitments you have made for yourself – powerful, focused intention gets powerful, noticeable results.

Tasks for the Week and Beyond

❖ Put the list of actions in your mission statement in a prominent place. Check this each week and renew it when necessary. Make sure these actions are geared to Specific Measurable Results (SMRs), so that you know when you have succeeded. Give yourself gold stars for results and some kind of extra-special treat when you achieved something you thought of as really difficult.

❖ Maintain regular contact with your guardian angel.

❖ When you feel in need of specific help, for particular occasions, ask one or more of the archangels.

❖ Meditate regularly.

❖ Set aside one day a week when you do the minimum of everyday things and give yourself time to reflect on the week that has passed. In our family we have a meal together on Friday night and we always ask each other 'What was the best thing that happened for you during the week?'

❖ Take time out in natural surroundings. Light a fire to warm your spirit; stand on a hilltop and feel the breezes, to clear your mind; find a brook, or go to the sea to soothe your heart; walk bare-foot on the earth to help you feel grounded and stable.

❖ When things go pear-shaped, when you feel in the doldrums and that nothing is going right, refer back to the four worlds and ask yourself these questions:

> FIRE Do I feel passionately enough about this project/activity/ career etc. to go the extra distance, to keep my focus on bringing my intention into the world?
>
> AIR Are my choices and plans consistent with bringing my intention into the world, or have I introduced other ideas that are distracting me?
>
> WATER Am I allowing negative feelings about my worth, or any sadness about past issues, to cloud my judgement or depress my energy?
>
> EARTH Are there any more actions I can take, that will help to manifest my vision in the world?

Whenever you have to say no to any of these questions, go back to the appropriate chapter and look through the exercises, repeating any that you think would help you.

❖ Complete the Review of Part 4 below.

REVIEW OF PART 4 – EARTH

Go back to the exercises you completed in the Earth stage, in Weeks 10, 11 and 12, then answer the following questions:

1 Are you using your time wisely?
2 Do you feel confident that you can use your gifts and talents in the world and bring about your soul's purpose? Are you in action, taking daily steps that support the manifestation of your intention?
3 Do you have complete trust in Divine love, in the invisible spiritual

---

powers and in your guardian angel, and know that you can and will manifest your intentions? Do you know, for certain, that the invisible power of Divine love supports you in creating whatever you choose?

If the answer to 1 is no, or if you feel a bit unsure about how you are using your time, do another time and motion study for a week. Then, return to the timetable exercise in Week 10, page 174. Repeat the exercise and create a new timetable.

If the answer to 2 is no, please return to Week 11 and repeat the exercise in which you list your gifts and talents. Then repeat the exercise where you make a list of actions that you can take, to bring your talent into the world.

If the answer to 3 is no, repeat the following affirmation at least once a day until you can answer yes, and then go back to it whenever you are feeling low in energy or confidence:

MY SOUL IS A SPARK OF DIVINE SPIRIT
MY MIND IS A FRAGMENT OF DIVINE INTELLIGENCE
MY HEART PULSES WITH DIVINE LOVE
AND DIVINE POWER WORKS WITH ME AND THROUGH ME TO
   MANIFEST
MY INTENTIONS IN THE WORLD.

Summary

It is not always easy to maintain your personal focus, especially if you spend time with family members or colleagues who are trudging along the same old weary-making path. Other people's attitudes can bring us down quite quickly. The bloke at the bus stop complains about public transport, the cleaning lady moans about her unrewarding job, your brother or sister loses their job – the everyday world is full of dissatisfied people and we can be so easily worn down by their comments. Be constantly alert and do not allow their complaints to penetrate your own, positive aura. And watch out for the 'candle-snuffers', the people who 'rain on your parade' when they see you making progress – counter their negativity with cheer-fulness and radiate your new energy towards them. Bless them in your meditations and make them a present of this book.

CLOSING DOWN

At the end of your session, sit quietly with your guardian angel. Visualise the things you have planned for the week ahead and for the near future. Project your mind and see yourself as you intend to be twelve months hence. Use the affirmation I gave you for the last two weeks and keep repeating it as often as you can: I AM THE CREATIVE POWER IN MY WORLD AND I INTEND TO UNFOLD MY LIFE'S PURPOSE FOR THE BENEFIT OF MY OWN SOUL AND FOR THE BENEFIT OF THOSE AROUND ME.

Epilogue

The rose adorns herself, in order to adorn the garden.
RUDOLF STEINER

Our vision should be to live with passion, carrying a flaming baton like an Olympic runner, as a light for those around us, which we can also pass on to those who follow.

So here are four rules for living:

FIRE Live with passion. Never let your fire be extinguished or suppressed by fear or dismay.

AIR Think beautiful thoughts and you will create beauty. Never allow the negative thoughts of other people or organisations (political, educational or commercial) to sway your belief in the goodness of the Divine power that creates all things.

WATER Love all creation, even the bits that seem unloveable – especially those. As the writer Henry James said, there are three rules: be kind, be kind, be kind.

EARTH Be in action to manifest your own soul's purpose for your present incarnation. Dare to be fully alive, take risks and make mistakes, knowing that most of the time, as the poet Rilke says, we have to live the questions, without expecting to get answers.

Remember, life is for living. Use your power, your wisdom and your love to create the best possibilities for yourself and others. None of us is perfect, and some times will be tougher than others, but your intentions are the driving force that will create your life, so make sure you are focussed and committed to living a great life.

Life is no 'brief candle' to me. It is a sort of splendid torch that I have got hold of for the moment, and I want to make it burn as brightly as possible before handing it on to future generations.

GEORGE BERNARD SHAW

Shalom

Appendix 1

The Archangels

Everything in creation is based on energy and the angels and archangels hold the creative patterns together. If you think of a piece of soft, shapeless fabric, then this is how creative energy would be without the angelic builders. You could say they are like the pins or stitches that hold a piece of fabric in place when you create a garment. The material, solid world, is a manifestation of pure energy, which vibrates at higher or lower speeds and gives rise to everything we experience, whether it is rock-hard solid, or fluid like water, or transparent like air. There are vast numbers of archangels, who are guardians of the many, many levels of vibration in creation.

The Archangels and the Rays of Divine Light

The archangels are often associated with the seven rays or coloured flames. You may already have come across the idea that the white light of the Divine power divides itself into seven colours, just as white light travelling through a prism creates a rainbow. This knowledge was being circulated in the late nineteenth and early twentieth centuries when three great Western women compiled huge books dealing with the hidden secrets of creation. I call these ladies the Busy Bees because their names all began with B: Mme H.P. Blavatsky (1831–91), Annie Besant (1847–1933) and Alice Bailey (1880–1949). These esoteric researchers believed that a treasure house of ancient wisdom and knowledge had been dispersed across the world at the time of the deluge.* They believed that all religions, especially the mystical traditions such as yoga, the Kabbalah, Sufism and so on, were essentially telling us the same thing in different ways. They planned to contribute to the enlightenment of humanity by collating these spiritual treasures, channelled to them from discarnate 'masters'.

The idea of the seven rays can be found in Alice Bailey's book, *The Treatise on the Seven Rays*, first published in 1936. Although Alice Bailey does not mention the archangels, I believe they are guardians of the rays, which can also be thought of as cosmic filaments or strands, vibrations which enable the pure white light of Divine power to become manifest in our everyday reality. The mystical insights of the ancients seem to resonate with modern quantum physics, in which 'super-string' theory, like Kabbalistic cosmology, has ten dimensions.

All three esoteric teachers incorporated wisdom from the Kabbalah, the Jewish mystical tradition, into their writings. The Kabbalistic Tree of Life describes the way the light and energy of Divine power divides and separates, flowing through channels and collecting in containers, called *sefirot* (Figure 7). There are seven of these containers in the lower part of the Tree, and three in the higher part, divided by a magical, non-*sefira*, known as the holy spirit (*Ruah ha Kodesh*, the holy breath). Similarly, Alice Bailey calls the seven rays the 'creative builders'.

The seven lower *sefirot* in the Kabbalah are also referred to as the gates of light, and each one has an archangel associated with it, as a guardian or keeper of the gate. Figure 8 shows the traditional placement of these archangels.

---

* At the present time we do not have definite evidence of the existence of ancient civilisations, such as Atlantis and Lemuria, but we know that so-called myths invariably have some fairly large grains of truth in them. Consistent stories, from a variety of civilisations, suggest that there really was a flood, or a deluge, and that ancient civilisations may have been swept away at that time.

Figure 7

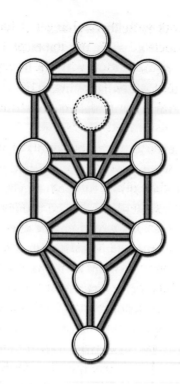

Figure 8

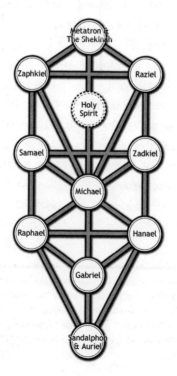

During my inner work with the archangels I have experienced an eighth archangel associated with the lower part of the Tree*. This came when I asked in meditation why the fourth great archangel, Auriel, was not included on the Tree of Life. The answer came quickly in a clear vision. Auriel, I was told, was the 'bride' of the Archangel Sandalphon, who is also called the Messiah. Sandalphon is said to have come to earth as the prophet Elijah and it is when Elijah appears again that we will know the Messianic Age has arrived. As the most grounded of the archangels, standing at the foot of the tree, Sandalphon works to ground the heavenly ideal on Earth. But he does need a companion in order for this new stage of life to be balanced – a bride to carry the feminine energy. This, I was told, is where Auriel can be found. She carries the eighth ray, which is silver.

At the top of the Tree you will see that the Great Angel Metatron has his own companion, the Shekinah.† Kabbalistic tradition tells us that the Shekinah is the feminine aspect of God, the Divine presence, who hid herself from humanity when Adam and Eve were expelled from the Garden of Eden. When humans begin to rediscover the Divine presence in creation, then the Shekinah will reappear, walking beside her bridegroom, the Messiah.

THE MYSTERIOUS Ms

If you look at the map of the Tree of Life, you will see that the central pillar is headed by Metatron; in the centre is Michael and at the foot is Sandalphon, the Messiah – three Ms. But there are two other Ms who play a part in bringing wisdom to humanity.

The fourth M is Melchizedek, the high priest who inaugurated the celebration of Divine love by using bread and wine. His name is derived from two Hebrew words *melech* and *tzadik*, meaning king

---

* You will see from Figure 8 that there are archangels above The Holy Spirit as well, but we are not dealing with them in this book. There are, of course, many other archangels, apart from those who play these key roles in creation. For lots more archangels, consult Gustav Davidson: *A Dictionary of Angels* (see on page 219).

† Jophiel, or Iofiel (the Hebrew name begins with the letter 'yod'), whose name means 'beauty of God', is also described as a companion to Metratron.

or ruler, and righteous.* He is said to have been king of Salem, the old name for Jerusalem.† Melchizedek is not included on the Tree of Life and is not openly described as an angel but it is said that he had no father or mother, and no 'days or years', so he must be thought of as some kind of supernatural emissary who took human form.‡ Old texts tell us that Melchizedek was either the son (Shem) of Noah, or Noah's nephew, by Noah's brother Nir. And Noah's grandfather was the fifth M, the famous Methuselah, who entrusted Melchizedek with the ancient wisdom known to humanity before the flood.

Hebrew texts tell us that Metatron and Michael are the same angel – the great angel. Metatron worked on Earth as the prophet Enoch, who was consumed by fire when he returned to the celestial realms. Michael appeared as a prince to the prophet Daniel, to help the house of Israel against its enemies.§

So we can think of the five Ms as heavenly emissaries. Whether archangels or prophets, they work towards opening the central pillar of the Tree of Life in order to bring heaven down to Earth. Their presence, in heaven and on Earth, encourages us to raise our state of consciousness so that we become open to receiving the mystical gift of heavenly insight. The bread (Earth) and wine (heaven) in the Christian communion and the Jewish kiddush remind us of the ritual inaugurated by Melchizedek. Many writers believe that the arrival of Melchizedek foreshadowed the coming of Jesus, who has also been referred to as the great angel.¶

The Archangels and Your Life Purpose

When you have discovered your own basic purpose you will be able to work with an archangel who will naturally support you because

---

* This event happened in the time of Abraham, see Genesis 14:18–20.
† But Salem, as in *shalom*, means peace, so being king of Salem may have meant being a peaceful king, rather than king of a particular place.
‡ Hebrews 5:10.
§ Daniel 10:13.
¶ Psalm 110:4.

his or her own Divine nature resonates with your purpose. You can also ask any of the others for help with a particular issue. Below are listed the chief characteristics of the eight great archangels.

Leading

MICHAEL – golden ray – the Sun – rules the world of creative intention: fire, supported by the seraphim, whose constant hymn of 'Holy, holy, holy', maintains the Divine fire. Michael's name means 'like unto God'.

Michael is the leader of the archangels. He leads by providing clear vision and inspiration. If your purpose is to lead, Michael is your natural ally. He also rules the element of fire and anyone who wishes to reconnect with their passion and enthusiasm will find him a powerful support.

   Keywords: courage, sovereignty, leadership, commitment, honour, faith

---

INVOCATION TO MICHAEL
Michael, teach me to lead with a true vision and with clarity. Remind me that the best leader is a servant and allow me to set aside my personal fears and anxieties so that I can maintain my purpose and fulfil my destiny.

Creating

GABRIEL – yellow ray – mercury – rules the world of information: air, supported by the other archangels, who help to shape plans and ideas. Gabriel's name means 'strength of God'.

Gabriel is a creator, bringing music, poetry, wisdom and messages of change and growth. If your purpose is to create, Gabriel will be your companion. He also rules the element of air and anyone who is working with new ideas, or going through a process of change will find Gabriel an inspiring helper.

Keywords: change, messages, spiritual growth, signs, guidance

---

INVOCATION TO GABRIEL

Gabriel, teach me to listen to the creative voice within my mind and to discern the true message of my soul. Help me bring beauty, joy and wisdom into the world and allow me to create in a spirit of generosity, seeking to share without thought of personal gain.

Healing

RAPHAEL – violet ray – Venus – rules the world of nurturing: water. He networks with all the angels to heal the Earth, so that it will be a suitable home for humanity. Raphael's name means 'healing of God.'

Raphael is the healer. If your purpose is to heal, Raphael will help you to cast out negativity and support you when you are dealing with gremlins, whether yours or those of your clients. Anyone in need of healing, or wanting to offer help to others in need of healing, can work with Raphael's gentle and reassuring energy.

Keywords: reassurance, harmony, reconciliation, healing, love

---

INVOCATION TO RAPHAEL

Raphael, I want to work as a healer, and I understand that Divine love heals all things. Help me open myself to the constant flow of this love. Remind me, day by day, that we are all connected and help me clear the blocks that get in the way of love and healing.

Protecting and Nurturing

AURIEL – silver ray – the Moon, and SANDALPHON – green ray – the Earth – together rule the world of manifestation: Earth. These two archangels work with the devas and nature spirits to maintain and protect our planet. Auriel's name means 'light of God'. Sandalphon's name suggests the sound of footsteps on the Earth*.

Auriel and Sandalphon are protectors and nurturers. If this is your purpose in life, choose to work with either or both of these archangels. Auriel brings intuition, Sandalphon is more practical. They will, of course, support anyone who feels in need of protection or guidance, or who wishes to work with nature.

Keywords for Auriel: mother-love, peace, grace, tender loving care

Keywords for Sandalphon: trust, reliability, stewardship, guidance, manifestation

---

INVOCATION TO AURIEL

Auriel, help me to bring nurturing and support to all those that I meet. Let the light of God shine through me as I walk in this world and let all my actions be based on integrity, faith and service.

INVOCATION TO SANDALPHON

Sandalphon, help me to protect and nurture all creatures, great and small, and work with the Divine powers to maintain the beauty of creation. Remind me to tread softly wherever I go.

Transforming

HANAEL – red ray – Mars – Hanael's name means 'he who sees God' (he is sometimes called Chamuel, meaning 'he who seeks God'.[†]

---

* Most of the archangels have Hebrew names. The suffix *el* means 'of God'. Sandalphon's name, like Metatron's name, is not Hebrew, but Greek, and I have not yet found out why this should be.

† When transliterating Hebrew, there is often some confusion between the sounds of 'h' and 'ch' (as in 'lo*ch*'). For example, we often call the Jewish festival of lights, which falls near Christmas, Hannukah, but the Hebrew letter at the beginning of this word is actually pronounced 'ch', so we should really say 'Channukah'.

Hanael is a warrior archangel, encouraging transformation at all levels: personal, social, political and planetary.

Hanael is the transformer. If you have this purpose, then Hanael will be at your side through thick and thin. Invoke his help when you need more vitality, or if you need to be powerful, rather than forceful, in achieving your ends. Anyone in need of a dynamic pick-me-up can call on Hanael and feel re-energised.

Keywords: energy, direction, purpose, assertiveness, vitality

---

INVOCATION TO HANAEL

Hanael, I want to contribute to the transformation of the world. I need to use my assertive drives for the benefit of people I meet and I am looking for opportunities to encourage change and commitment in all spheres of life. Remind me, on a daily basis, that change unfolds best through constant, loving persistence, not by force.

Organising

SAMAEL – blue ray – Saturn – Samael has a difficult name. 'Sam' in Hebrew means 'poison', and Samael is considered to be the same angel as Satan. In old Hebrew texts, Satan is not a wicked or fallen angel, but a tester, who shows humanity that God's will is inscrutable and that sometimes we just have to get on with life, even if it is not going our way. So Samael/Satan is there to tell us that however much we organise life to our own design, there may be an invisible factor that takes the result out of our hands.

Samael is the organiser. Satan has been described as the prideful angel. Perhaps people who organise well are also most susceptible to hubris or pride. The great temptation is to become a controller. When you work with Samael, be constantly aware that all your planning and organisation, however carefully conceived, is still reliant on creative forces beyond your control. Then Divine power will work through you, not for you.* Samael will work with anyone who is going through a testing time, and will help them see the positive value of trials and tribulations.

Keywords: structure, testing, limitation, responsibility

INVOCATION TO SAMAEL

Samael, my purpose in life is to be an organiser, providing structures that allow creative plans to develop and become manifested, for the benefit of all creation. Teach me how to develop a sense of appropriate limitation, so that I can work with respect for other people and for the whole of creation.

Teaching

ZADKIEL – indigo ray – Jupiter – Zadkiel's name means 'righteousness of God'. He is an angel of benevolence, mercy and abundance. When you have gained mastery over your ego, Zadkiel gives you a cup overflowing with Divine treasures – wisdom, knowledge and the peace that passes all understanding.

Zadkiel is the teacher. True teaching is an act of great generosity. The best kind of teacher is someone who develops his or her own wisdom and knowledge, not just for personal benefit, but in order to share it with others. Every teacher is a life-long student, always questing after new insights to pass on to others. If you are a natural teacher, then Zadkiel will make sure that you are drawn to the best sources of human understanding and will bring you dreams and messages from the heavenly realms. Anyone who seeks knowledge to support their purpose can work with Zadkiel.

Keywords: abundance, generosity, enthusiasm, confidence

---

* You will remember how Satan tempted Jesus to use Divine power for himself. Satan is God's way of making sure we do not overstep the boundaries of our human ability.

INVOCATION TO ZADKIEL

Zadkiel, I wish to be a teacher, bringing wisdom and knowledge into the world. Yet I also know I have a great deal to learn myself. Remind me as I grow in confidence, never to assume that I have all the answers and help me to be open always to new vision and fresh insights.

For information about the other archangels on the Tree of Life and for your solar archangel (who rules your zodiac sun sign and can also be a supporter for your purpose), see my book *Living with Angels* (Recommendations page 219).

Appendix 2

A Bedtime Prayer to the Four Archangels

I have developed this visualisation from a Jewish bedtime prayer. The idea is to surround yourself with the archangels, who create a protective force field around you as you sleep. The placement of the archangels has been changed from the traditional version, when I quoted in *Living with Angels*. I find these new placements feel more comfortable – as long as all four are around you it probably doesn't matter where they are. So, if you have problems with lefts and rights, don't worry!

> *May Gabriel be at my right side, to guide my hand and my words*
> *May Raphael be at my left side, to heal me and help me bring healing to others*
> *May Auriel be behind me, so that I may rest in her soft and tender care*
> *May Michael be in front of me, as a shield for my heart and to lead me forward*
> *And above my head may the Shekinah, the Divine presence, bring me close to heaven as I sleep.*

As this is a bedtime visualisation do not light a candle, as you are likely to drift off to sleep and leave it burning. As a preparation, if you have a copy of *The Angels' Script* (see page 222), you could use the appropriate archangel cards – Michael, Gabriel, Raphael, Auriel and the Shekinah – and place them beside or around your bed.

If you fall asleep before completing the process, don't worry. The fact that you went to bed with the intention of calling the archangels will automatically bring them close to your energy field. The next morning you will still feel their presence as you go about your daily business.

❖ When you get into bed, lie on your back, close your eyes and breathe gently but deeply, allowing your whole body to relax. Notice any parts of your body that are tense and allow them to become heavy as you sink more deeply into a state of relaxation.

❖ Imagine a presence at the right side of your face and body. This may feel like a tingling vibration or a cool breeze. If you cannot feel a sensation, just imagine that a presence is near you, close to your body, almost touching your right side: the archangel GABRIEL, the messenger of Divine, who brings change into your life. Gabriel may bring a dream for you, encouraging you to renew your life and realise your potential.

❖ When you are ready, do the same for the left side of your body, imagining the close presence of RAPHAEL, the archangel of healing. Now you can feel protected on both sides by the two archangels.

❖ Allow yourself to feel the presence of something beneath you, holding you up, supporting you from underneath. This is AURIEL, the tender light of the Divine.

❖ Above your body, hovering over the length of your face, torso and limbs, a bright light is shining. Allow it to be as bright as you can. Think of this presence as MICHAEL, the archangel of the sun, of the heart, of courage. Now you are surrounded on all four sides, with courage, with a messenger, with healing and with tenderness.

❖ Finally, imagine a huge benevolent cloud hovering above your head. This is the SHEKINAH, the feminine presence of the Divine. She is hidden in the darkness but gradually reveals her pure light to the spiritual seeker. Allow the clear light of the Shekinah to descend slowly, surrounding you and enveloping you with loving protection and unconditional love, cradling you in the softest, most peaceful state of mind you have ever experienced. Surrounded by the four greatest archangels and the Shekinah, you are in the arms of infinite kindness, absolute security and safety.

Appendix 3

Remedies, Oils and Crystals

You may find it helpful to use some of the products listed below, to lift your mood and/or raise the atmosphere of your room. For fuller information about their use, see the Recommendations on page 219.

Bach Flower Remedies

There are 39 Bach Flower Remedies in all. I recommend the following as particularly useful for certain stages of your journey:

> For calming the mind: *White Chestnut*
> For grounding, if you feel a little spaced out: *Clematis*
> For anxiety: *Rock rose*
> For anger and sadness: Rescue Remedy

Essential Oils

Always buy good quality oils, not the pre-mixed kind. Use one or two drops in the bath, or diluted in almond oil on your pulses and throat. You can also use them in a vaporiser in the room where you are working with your guardian angel. Choose whatever is appropriate for you from the following:

Cedarwood is good for grounding
Chamomile brings inner peace
Frankincense brings inspiration and faith
Lavender clears negative thoughts and brings inner guidance

Marjoram calms the mind and emotions

Neroli reduces fear and opens the heart

Patchouli helps you feel strongly grounded

Rose opens the heart

Sandalwood quietens the mind and assists meditation

Crystals and Gemstones

You can place these in your space while you are working with your guardian angel, beside your bed or under your pillow at night. You can also hold the appropriate one while working on a particular issue. Crystals and stones need cleansing regularly, especially if you are releasing negativity. You can hold them under cold running water, or soak them for an hour or two in a solution of salt and water. Don't use a towel to dry them: let them dry naturally in sunlight or moonlight, when they will absorb the natural energies of sun or moon.

Amber protects, purifies and changes negative energy into positive; it is used by Native Americans and in Asia as a sacred talisman.

Amethyst is protective and helps meditation.

Blue lace agate calms the mind and soothes the emotions; helps to open consciousness.

Boji stone is grounding and promotes telepathy.

Carnelian is grounding and increases inner receptivity.

Chalcedony quartz is solid and grounding.

Fire agate is an aid to memory.

Green moss is good for centring and self-esteem.

Hematite, one of the most grounding of stones, brings mental clarity and aids concentration and memory.

Jade assists dream work when placed under the pillow.

Lapis lazuli is for mental calm; connecting heart and mind, it increases psychic ability and opens connections for higher guidance.

Obsidian is for detachment and grounding.

Picture agate improves visualisation by co-ordinating left and right brain activity during meditation.

Rose quartz is for peacefulness, forgiveness, self-love and easing loss.

Sapphire amplifies intuitive ability, clears mental clutter.

Snakeskin agate encourages inner peace.

Silver leaf is a stone of abundance which is protective and grounding.

Sodalite is for communication; helps with logic, ideas and truth.

Tourmaline is protective and grounding.

Turquoise is protective, good for serenity, absorbs negativity and brings wisdom.

Recommendations

Books & Audio

Bolles, Richard, *What Color is Your Parachute?*, Berkeley, California: Ten Speed Press, published annually

Byron, Katie, *Loving What Is*, London: Rider, 2002

Cameron, Julia, *The Artist's Way*, London: Pan Books, 1995

Cameron, Julia, *Vein of Gold*, London: Pan Macmillan, 1997

Chopra, Deepak, *Ageless Body, Timeless Mind*, London: Rider, 1993

Chopra, Deepak, *How to Know God*, New York: Rider, 2000

Cortens, Theolyn, *Living with Angels*, London: Piatkus, 2003

Cortens, Theolyn, *The Angels' Script (2nd* edition), London: Soul School Publishing, 2004

Davidson, Gustav, *A Dictionary of Angels*, London: Simon & Schuster, 1994

Ford, Debbie, *The Dark Side of the Light Chasers*, London: Hodder & Stoughton, 2001

Ford, Debbie, *The Secret of the Shadow*, London: Hodder & Stoughton, 2002

Gray, John, *How to Get What You Want, and Want What You've Got*, London: Vermilion, 1999

Hall, Judy, *The Crystal Bible*, London: Godsfield, 2003

Myss, Caroline, *Sacred Contracts*, London: Bantam, 2002

Myss, Caroline, *Self Esteem*, four CDs by Sounds True, Boulder, Colorado, 2002

Rogers, Jane, *Breaking Free* (book and CD), Oxford: Living Well Publications, 2000

Watts, Alan, *The Book on the Taboo Against Knowing Who You Are*, London: Jonathon Cape, 1969

Music for the Four Worlds

Music is a personal matter and no doubt you have your own favourites. But here are some suggestions for the four different stages in the course:

FIRE Find heart-stirring music, such as Handel's *Entrance of the Queen of Sheba*, Elgar's *Jerusalem*, Tchaikovsky's *1812* Overture or any of those great classics that people play at firework concerts. When the picnic season arrives go to one.

AIR Use mind-expanding music with patterns and structures, such as Bach's Fugues, and music for wind instruments, such as Mozart's Clarinet Concertos. Any music that uses the flute will help.

WATER Listen to soothing, melodic music, such as Debussy's piano music and Beethoven's *Moonlight Sonata*. Music played on the lute or classical guitar provides a nurturing, angelic atmosphere.

EARTH Move to suitable, grounding music – have a good stomp. Choose music with a lively rhythm and beat, especially if it has lots of drums and percussion. Try folk or circle-dance music, especially Middle Eastern, Greek and Mongolian; or dance to your favourite rock and pop music.

Websites

If you find that doing this course leads you to considering a change of vocation or lifestyle, the Internet is an invaluable resource for finding out what is out there, how to re-qualify, pay scales and so on. You may want to develop your own website, or use the Internet to make contact with others of like mind.

For general career or job searching try:

www.notaproperjob.co.uk
www.jobhuntersbible.com – this is a supplement to Richard Bolles's excellent guide to changing career, *What Color is Your Parachute?*, published annually since 1972. Both the book and the site offer plenty of useful guidelines to anyone, anywhere, who is re-evaluating their life.

Newspapers for Your Birth Date

There are several companies around, and you can research these on the Internet. Some are expensive, so shop around. The company I have used is:

Papers Past
Chapel Row
Truro
Cornwall TR1 2EA
Tel: 01872 261 220
Website: www.paperspast.co.uk

At the time of writing the cost of one paper is £19.99 including the standard postage and packaging service, which can take up to 28 days but is usually much quicker. Your newspaper comes in a cardboard presentation box, but if you are giving it as a present a leather wallet is available for an extra £10. Ian Willsher, who runs Papers Past, was very helpful at the last minute when I wanted a 1924 newspaper for my mother's eightieth birthday.

The Chalice Well

This is one of the oldest continually used holy wells in Britain. To be at the well head, to drink the water and absorb the atmosphere of the place, is an inspiring experience. The gardens are also wonderful to visit.

The Chalice Well
Chilkwell Street
Glastonbury
Somerset
BA6 8DD
Tel: 01458 831154
Website: www.chalicewell.org.uk

Soul School Courses and The Angels' Script

Workshops and Home Study Courses

Theolyn Cortens offers workshops and home study courses to spiritual seekers in the UK and abroad. Her students include an engineer, a GP, Reiki healers, hairdressers, cabin crew members on a cruise liner, and others from many more walks of life. They live in many countries around the world; the oldest student so far is 86 and the youngest is 12. All Theolyn's home study students report that Soul School courses bring inspiration and transformation: students change their careers, relationships in the home improve and they recognise a new lightness and joy in their everyday lives.

For more information about Theolyn's home study courses contact:

Soul School,
PO Box 338873,
London
N8 3FY
Tel: 0845 458 0628
Website: www.soulschool.co.uk

The Angels' Script

The Angels' Script is a set of 36 cards with angelic messages, to guide you on your life path. *The Script* is based on messages channelled by Theolyn and is a major teaching tool in Theolyn's courses.

In ancient times mystics used symbols to open up their inner channels in order to communicate with the angels. Their symbols were often developed from the written alphabet, which was held to be magical and holy. Both Hebrew and Sanskrit are regarded as sacred languages, and in both languages the actual shape of the letters carries spiritual power. *The Writing of the Angels*, which Theolyn used to access the messages in *The Script*, is one of these symbolic alphabets, based on Hebrew, which has been used by mystics through the ages. No one knows exactly how it originated, but we do know that it was used by Kabbalists in Renaissance Europe, who claimed it had been handed down from King Solomon.

King Solomon lived 3,000 years ago, in Israel, and was known to have been a great seeker after wisdom. Solomon shared this interest with the famous Queen of Sheba, and it is quite probable that they worked together to preserve the ancient knowledge. They had both been in close contact with the Babylonians, who had developed their wisdom by communing with the spirits of the stars and planets. It is likely that *The Writing of the Angels* was part of this heritage. In 1993, after a past-life experience, Theolyn discovered the alphabet in an old book about angels, and channelled a series of messages, one for each symbol, which are published in *The Angels' Script*.

The Angels' Script, published by Soul School Publishing at £17.95, is available from Soul School (see address above) or from your local bookshop, ISBN 1–898632–05–7.

About the Author

Theolyn has studied metaphysical, religious and philosophical texts since her early teens. In 1974 she experienced a spontaneous and awe-inspiring spiritual awakening, when she was engulfed by a brilliant, golden light, accompanied by heavenly voices. Although it was many years before she understood or could put a name to this intense experience, it has since inspired her to teach people how to open their own inner gates and discover the heavenly realms for themselves.

Theolyn has had a wide variety of work experiences. She has worked as a technical draftsperson, a lawyer's secretary, a civil servant, a shop assistant, a theatrical costume designer and creator of ball gowns and wedding dresses, which were sold in Harrods and Liberty of London. In Glastonbury and in Oxfordshire she created events to celebrate the turning cycle of the seasons, helped people create ceremonies for rites of passage and edited local alternative magazines. Theolyn has also been an organiser for community education and for the Workers' Educational Association, and a creative writing tutor for Ruskin College, Oxford; she is an experienced and qualified adult education teacher, with an Honours Degree in Philosophy, Literature and Religion.

As well as writing angel books and running Soul School courses, Theolyn is researching the role of angels in the Jewish mystical text, *The Zohar* (The Book of Splendour) for her Master's degree, at the University of Wales, Lampeter. The University is the home of the Religious Experience Research Centre, originally set up in Oxford by Sir Alister Hardy to study the spiritual nature of humanity. The Research Centre has an archive of over 7,000 reports from people from all walks of life, who have contributed a record of their spiritual experiences. Theolyn has given papers at the annual Alister Hardy conferences, and recently developed an experiential event at the University called Spirituality and the Creative Arts, with her co-organiser Patricia Murphy.

Poetry and the creation of musical theatre are also high on Theolyn's agenda. Her poetry has been published in a number of anthologies including *Earth Ascending* (Stride Books, 1998, ed. Jay Ramsay); and she has privately published her own collections: *Flowers from the Galaxy* and *Baba Yaga and Other Tasty Morsels. Flowers from the Galaxy* includes several poems about her angel experiences. She is presently writing a cycle of poems about the search for *The Golden Fleece*. Theolyn is co-creator of the witty and inspiring musical *Roll over Jehovah!* with music and lyrics by Will, her husband, and script by Tim Jarman. *Roll over!* has already had one professional London production. She is presently collaborating with Will creating a musical based on the ancient myth of *Innana*, the sky goddess who descends into the underworld. Watch this space!

Theolyn has four daughters and five grandchildren. She lives in London with her husband and soul mate, Will, and their white cat, Cleopatra.

Index